240

S. E. Brynestad .
241 East 123 St
New York City
N. Y.

By William McDougall, F.R.S.

———

The Group Mind

Ethics and Some Modern World Problems

Ethics and Some Modern World Problems

By

William McDougall

Professor of Psychology in Harvard University
Author of "The Group Mind"

G. P. Putnam's Sons
New York & London
The Knickerbocker Press
1924

Made in the United States of America

PREFACE

An eminent and genial critic has recently described me as "an American Nietzschean reactionary." I do not wish to dispute the accuracy of this classification; nor do I complain against it; for I am not one of those who are carried away by every newest fad and fashion in science or philosophy or politics. I am well aware that the publication of this short series of lectures will provoke renewed outpourings of scorn from some of those who figure as exponents of the democratic principle, and that this little book will be described by them as an attack upon Democracy. I have learnt also that, in these days when all of us are beset by the difficulty of reading more than a small fraction of the interesting matter that pours from a thousand presses, even sympathetic readers too often fail to seize the essential import and intention of an author.

I therefore take this opportunity to assert

explicitly that I am, in principle and sympathy, a democrat. I do not regard democratic government as an end in itself; nor do I regard it as the only possible form of good government. For I have observed at close quarters within the British Empire that the working of a paternal autocracy may display justice, wisdom, and benevolence with more consistency than any democracy hitherto can claim to have achieved. Nor do I forget the judgment of Gibbon on the age of the Antonines: "The vast extent of the Roman Empire was governed by absolute power under the guidance of virtue and wisdom."

I am a democrat, because I see clearly that democracy, or government by public opinion, with all its faults and all its dangers, is the only form of government under which the nations of the earth can hope to go onward to higher levels of civilization, levels at which a life of reasonable dignity and happiness shall be within the reach of the great majority of mankind. But I do not believe that such progress may be ensured by the simple expedient of giving one vote to every adult human being and leaving the rest to Nature. The day may come when that simple formula may suffice; to hasten and ensure the coming of that day must be the supreme purpose of every sincere and not wholly selfish person.

Before the advent of that day of triumph for the democratic principle, our civilization must fight, in a life and death struggle, with many opposing forces, with the self-seeking of ruthless men and nations, with greed and cruelty, with sloth and levity and dishonesty in private and in public life.

The tragedy of our situation is that the greatest danger threatening our civilization arises from the working within us of the altruistic or benevolent impulse, that impulse which (as I have argued at length elsewhere) is a deeply rooted element of all normal human nature and the essential and only source of all true morality, of all truly ethical conduct, whether of men or nations. For the altruistic impulse prompts us to desire that every human being shall be free to exercise and satisfy every strong impulse proper to the human species, especially that strongest of all our impulses, the impulse to procreate our kind. Yet it is one of the ultimate and ineradicable disharmonies of human life (and the fact cannot be too strongly insisted upon at the present time) that such exercise and satisfaction are not compatible with the maintenance and progress of any civilization of a high type.

In those civilizations in which this "natural right" has been exercised without restraint, it has been, with rare exceptions, at the cost of an immense mass of human suffering and degradation, more especially on the part of women and children; of which suffering and degradation the leading features have always been infanticide, abortion, and a tremendous infant mortality. Only under the rarest conditions, which can never again be realized (such as those under which the early colonization of North America was effected) has the shadow of this disharmony been partially lifted from a fraction of civilized mankind.

But the suffering and degradation of a multitude of human beings is not the whole of the price to be paid for that free exercise of this "natural right" which our equally natural altruism prompts us to demand for every man and woman. In the present age such exercise threatens to demand an even higher price, namely, the progressive deterioration of the intellectual and moral fibre of the human race. This is the great danger which besets our civilization; and will beset it, no matter how successful may be our efforts to abolish war and cruel oppression.

For the enduring success of democratic institutions in any country presupposes a high level of intelligence and morality on the part of all, or the great majority, of the citizens of that country. It is doubtful whether any existing population has achieved the required level; and it is certain that none can afford to suffer any actual deterioration, if its hopes of continued progress are to have any prospect of realization.

Nor will a high average level of intelligence and morality in any people suffice to secure for it continued progress or even continuance on the plane already achieved. It is necessary also that every generation shall produce its due quota of men of exceptional endowments, men who in every sphere of national life shall be the leaders and inspirers of their fellows; men and women who, as the "salt of the earth," shall preserve it from corruption and who, by their creative activities, shall improve, refine, and increase the sum of human culture. For, as

George Eliot has said, "Not God Himself can make man's best, without best men to help Him."

Some of the existing peoples have shown themselves capable of attaining a modest average of intelligence and morality, and of producing in fair numbers men and women of such great natural endowments as enable them to play the creative role of leaders; and it is a fair presumption that these peoples are more capable of these two essential achievements than most of those that hitherto have not displayed these capacities in an equal degree. Hence, as Lord Bryce has said, "What we must desire in the interests of mankind at large is that the more highly civilized races should increase faster than the more backward, so as to enable the former to prevail not merely by force, but by numbers and amicable influence."

Further, the future of civilization depends upon the attainment by the leading nations of a higher level of international morality than any hitherto established. And it remains doubtful whether any existing people is capable of rising to and of steadily maintaining the required level of international morality. Hence, to quote Lord Bryce again, "The prospect of

improving the relations of states and peoples ✓
to one another depends ultimately upon the possibility of improving human nature itself. . . .
Can it be raised to and sustained at a higher
level than it has yet attained? That is the
great question." The thesis of this book is
that any system of ethics which ignores this
great question is inadequate to the needs of
our time.

That is the large topic which I have discussed
very briefly in these pages. The full treatment of it would require several volumes. My
excuse for publishing a discussion of it so condensed and inadequate is that, in the present
distracted state of the world, any publication
that may stimulate thought or contribute however slightly to a better understanding of the
parlous state in which we find ourselves is justified and should not be delayed by considerations which, in a more tranquil age, might well
demand a more deliberate procedure.

The briefer the treatment of a vast topic, the
more necessary is some aid to the reader in
following the course of the argument. I therefore attempt to present here the content of the
six following lectures in briefest possible out-

line. In the first and second lectures I draw
attention to a fact which seems to me of the
first importance for the understanding of our
western civilization and especially of its present
world-problems and which nevertheless has not,
I think, been sufficiently recognized by philosophers or historians: the fact, namely, that our
civilization has developed on a dual ethical
basis, has been governed by ethical principles
of two very different systems which have
never been harmonized, but rather have been in
perpetual conflict. These two conflicting systems of ethics are here called the National and
the Universal Systems.

In Chapters III and IV I go on to show that
neither system alone will suffice as the basis
of our civilization; that the National system,
unsoftened and unchecked by its rival, must
lead to such disasters as the recent world war;
that the Universal system, unmodified by the
recognition of the validity of the National
system, must lead to universal stagnation and
decay; that, therefore, the great need of our
time is some rational and effective synthesis
of the two systems.

In the concluding chapters, I make certain

suggestions towards such a synthesis, insisting
that any such system must make two principal
demands or political prescriptions: first, it will
prescribe a true Internationalism, an Internationalism consisting in a society or family
of strong and stable nations, each of which
shall conduct itself as a moral organism,
sensitive and benevolently sympathetic to the
just claims of each member of the family; secondly, it will prescribe for each nation such
political organization as will enable it effectively
to play its proper part among its fellow nations;
an organization which, while wholesomely democratic, in accordance with the dictates of Universal Ethics, shall yet give due recognition to
the aristocratic principle, as required by the
teaching of National Ethics.

The lectures are here printed substantially
as they were delivered. I have added a number
of footnotes and an appendix containing two
suggestions towards the better establishment
of international justice. Some readers who
may not care to read the philosophical discussions of the lectures may nevertheless be
interested in these two practical suggestions.
In the thinking out of this appendix, I have

enjoyed the collaboration of my friend and former pupil, Mr. N. D. Hirsch.

I heartily thank the Northwestern University, which, by its invitation to the Harris lectureship, stimulated me to attempt to put in order some reflexions that had long occupied my mind, and also the audience which listened, in a manner very gratifying to me, to six lectures delivered in the space of one week.

To readers unacquainted with my previously published books I would point out that this book is the ethical supplement to my psychological study of "The Group Mind," a book published by G. P. Putnam's Sons in the year 1920.

W. McD.

Silver Lake, New Hampshire,
September, 1923.

THE N. W. HARRIS LECTURES

were founded in 1906 through the generosity of Mr. Norman Wait Harris of Chicago, and are to be given annually. The purpose of the lecture foundation is, as expressed by the donor, "to stimulate scientific research of the highest type and to bring the results of such research before the students and friends of Northwestern University, and through them to the world. By the term 'scientific research' is meant scholarly investigation into any department of human thought or effort without limitation to research in the so-called natural sciences, but with a desire that such investigation should be extended to cover the whole field of human knowledge."

CONTENTS

"Not God Himself can make man's best
Without best men to help Him."

GEORGE ELIOT.

"What we must desire in the interests of mankind at
large is that the more highly civilized races should increase faster than the more backward, so as to enable the
former to prevail not merely by force, but by numbers
and amicable influence."—VISCOUNT BRYCE.

"The prospect of improving the relations of states and
peoples to one another depends ultimately upon the
possibility of improving human nature itself. . . . Can
it be raised to and sustained at a higher level than it has
yet attained? That is the great question."

VISCOUNT BRYCE.

Ethics and Some Modern World Problems

Ethics and Some Modern World Problems

LECTURE I

THE TWO SYSTEMS OF ETHICS, THE UNIVERSAL AND THE NATIONAL

IN this short series of lectures, I propose to invite your attention to certain ethical and political problems which are already confronting the modern world and which promise to become very rapidly more urgent. They are problems which will have to be met by political action on the widest scale in the near future, political action which, if it is to be carried through successfully and confidently for the settlement of the problems I speak of, must conform to principles recognized as right or ethical. Yet they are problems in the face of which the ethical principles commonly accepted by civilized mankind give us no sure guidance. This is true, not only

3

of Christian or Western civilization, but also of most other civilizations of the present and the past.

The ethical principles of all these civilizations have had much in common, in spite of differences in detail and of emphasis. We like to claim, and I believe the claim is not without all foundation, that the civilization of Christendom has, thanks to the influence of its religion, accepted and in some measure practised a higher ethical code than any other. Yet, if we compare the Christian code with the moral codes of ancient Egypt, Greece or Rome, of China, of Japan, of the Moslem world, or of the Buddhist peoples, we find that in all these codes the most essential and effective precepts are substantially identical, in so far as they bear upon the personal relations of man to man.

To speak the truth, to be mutually helpful and loyal, to be compassionate, to do no violence to the persons or property of our neighbors, to practise moderation and self-discipline —these are the common stock of ethical precepts, without the cultivation of which, as a strong and effective moral tradition, no civilization can rise above a very crude level. No doubt the various civilizations have emphasized differently these main precepts; each may have insisted upon certain detailed applications in a manner peculiar to itself; and such special features of its moral code may have profoundly affected the course and destiny of each civilization. Perhaps we do not commonly realize how great a part such peculiarities of the moral codes have played in determining the fates of nations and of civilizations. Yet, in the main, the differences, as regards personal conduct of man to man, have been differences of the moral sanctions rather than differences of precept.

A further common feature of all the historic moral codes is that they have been (with certain partial exceptions to be noted presently) codes regulating the conduct of individuals in their intercourse with one another, and have had little or nothing to say concerning the relations of group to group, the intercourse of tribe with tribe, of nation with nation.

If we turn from the codes of practical ethics by which men have lived, and by which civilizations and nations have risen and fallen, to the reasonings and speculations of the moral philosophers, we find a corresponding state of affairs. In the main, the moral philosophers have been concerned to define more exactly the true ethical end, the nature of that good which is assumed to be the final goal of ethical endeavor, to refine the current precepts and practices which are the means towards that goal, and to discover the rational sanctions for such precepts and practices. They also, with few exceptions, have been content to discuss the relations of man to man and of the individual to the society into which he is born a member, neglecting those larger ethical problems which arise as soon as one well-defined human group comes into active relations with another.

In short, ethics, both practical and theoretical, popular and philosophical, has been in the main the ethics of the individual.

It is true that some of the ethical systems of the past have given prominence to the relations of the individual to his group considered as a whole, as a living entity with a life, a history, and a destiny of its own, an organism that is more than the sum of the individuals who compose it at each moment of time. And here we find the one important feature that differentiates all ethical systems into two great classes. In this respect, I say, we may properly divide all ethical codes and systems, both popular and philosophical, into two classes, the class of Universal Ethics, and the class of National Ethics, ethics of the group, of the tribe, nation, or State. To the former class belong the ethics of Christianity and of Buddhism, and less strictly the ethics of Mohammedanism. Each of these codes is bound up with a religion that aspires to universal dominion; each therefore claims that its rules of conduct are valid for and binding upon all men, and seeks to bring all mankind under the sway of such rules.

On the other hand, the ethical systems of Judaism, of Japan, of China, of Brahmanism, have been national systems; the outlook of each of these systems has been confined to a particular race or nation. And their aim has been, not only to control the conduct of men in relation to one another and for the sake of the welfare and happiness of individuals, but also to regulate the lives of men in relation to the nation or the State; their prescriptions, aiming at the welfare of individuals, have been modified and complicated by others designed to promote the welfare and the stability of the national group.

This difference may be described by saying that the systems of the one class are universal and individualist, while those of the other are national and political. The difference, the contrast, is illustrated vividly when we compare the ethics of Christianity with the ethics of Judaism.

The Jewish State was a theocracy, and the Jewish people worshipped a national God; their ethical precepts aimed, not only to regulate the conduct of men to one another, in their private relations as individuals, but also and especially to secure the prosperity and the perpetuation of the chosen people, as a national group distinct from all others. The ethical principles of Judaism were ethico-political. On the other hand, the non-political character of the ethics of Christianity was prescribed by its Founder in the command, "Render unto Cæsar the things that are Cæsar's." And, though the various Christian Churches have in later times become affiliated with various States, and though their ethical teaching has been in consequence complicated in some degree by political considerations, the non-political character of the earlier and purer form of Christianity was so well-marked as to provoke the resentment of the Roman State.

In this respect, the ethics of Greece and of Rome were peculiar. In both cases, the popular, the practical, ethical code by which the mass of men lived was essentially ethico-political; for their gods were national gods, and popular ethics and its sanctions were national. The moral philosophers of those States, on the other hand, taught ethical principles and precepts of universal validity; yet they were so far influenced by the spirit of nationality or statehood, by the spirit of national exclusiveness, that they seldom sought to apply their universal principles to the relations of men outside the limits of their own group. Their ethical principles claimed to be generally valid for all men; but the only men generally recognized as men in the full sense were their free fellow-citizens. Their slaves, even those of similar race, as well as the men of other races and nations, remained for the most part outside their purview.

Hence these philosophers failed to achieve any

synthesis of ethical and of political principles that could have general validity.

In the most famous of the philosophical writings of antiquity, the "Republic of Plato," ethics and politics were treated as inseparably combined in a single philosophical discipline. And, since the revival of learning, the "Republic" has been widely celebrated and studied. Yet the political ethics of Plato was gravely defective by reason of the restriction of his outlook to the free men of the Greek city-states; and the influence of the non-political Christian ethics had become dominant throughout western civilization during the middle ages. Hence, in spite of the protests of so great a man as Edmund Burke, who boldly proclaimed that "the principles of true politics are but those of morals enlarged," the western world has in the main continued to regard ethics and politics as two distinct studies[1]; and the whole world has

---

[1] The fact is illustrated by the division customary in our universities, where ethics and politics are represented by distinct chairs, and are not uncommonly assigned to two distinct faculties or divisions of the university. In his "History of Ethics," Henry Sidgwick, after defining Ethics as "the study of the ultimate Good of Man," wrote as follows: "In the definition above given, Ethics is not yet clearly distinguished from Politics; for Politics is also concerned with the Good or Welfare of men, so far as they are members of states.

continued to be divided between the two kinds
of ethical systems, the universal individualist systems and the national or ethico-political systems.

Let us pause here to contemplate the influence
of ethical systems of these two opposed types

And in fact the term Ethics is sometimes used, even by modern
writers, in a wide sense, so as to include at least a part of Politics—
viz., the consideration of the ultimate end or Good of the state, and
the general standard or criterion for determining the goodness or
badness of political institutions.   It is, however, also current in a
narrower sense—equivalent to the qualified term "Private Ethics,"
which is sometimes preferred—as a study of the Good or Wellbeing of
man, so far as this is attainable by the rational activity of individuals
as such.   This latter is the meaning to which the term is, in the
main, restricted in the historical sketch that follows; at the same
time I have not tried to draw a sharp division between the two subjects, the connection of which, in many at least of the systems with
which we have to deal, is conceived as very close and intimate.   The
difficulty of separating them is easily seen, whether we approach
the boundary between them from the ethical or from the political
side. . . .   Still we may, to a great extent, study the elements and
conditions of the good of individual men, so far as it is attainable
by the rational activity of themselves or other individuals acting as
private persons, without considering the manner in which the structure and functions of government should be determined with a view
to the same end; it is, then, to the former of these subjects, as distinct from the latter, that attention will be primarily directed in
the following pages " (page 3).

The foregoing passage shows how this eminent authority, who
wrote political treatises hardly less famous than his two books on
Ethics, continued to observe the artificial conventional distinction
between Ethics and Politics which had long been accepted by
most European philosophers and which has been a great source of
weakness in so much ethical discussion.   The persistence of the distinction is grounded in the prevalence of individualistic psychology
and the neglect to recognize the fact that a nation is a mental and
moral organism, a state of affairs which I have attempted to remedy
by writing "The Group Mind."

upon the fate of peoples. A national or political ethical system makes for extreme conservatism, for national stability and endurance. It tends to the preservation of the national type, not only by inculcating respect and reverence for the national gods and other national institutions, but also by preserving in some degree the racial purity of the people; for such a system is indifferent to the making of converts, it inspires no missionary enterprizes; it is adverse to intermarriage with aliens, and generally adverse also to the admission of aliens to the privileges of citizenship. These effects we see illustrated by the history of China, of Japan, and of Judaism.

China is the supreme example of endurance among nations; and of that endurance the ethical creed, with its worship of the emperor, its reverence for ancestors, its cult of the family and its hostility to foreign influences, has been, we may feel sure, a main condition, a condition which has preserved the people as a great nation, with all the essentials of its culture, through many centuries, in spite of vast natural calamities of plague and flood and war, and in spite of the lack of natural science and the correlative

of that lack, the flourishing of many gross super-
stitions. Japan repeats the history of China
on a smaller scale.

Even more striking illustration of the same
influence is afforded by the history of the
Jewish people. For there, in the absence of
every other condition favorable to national
survival, the influence of a strictly national
ethical code, backed by strong religious sanctions, has sufficed to preserve the people; and,
although they were few in numbers, were scattered widely over the face of the earth, and had
no national home, it has kept for them something
of the character of a nation.

If Greece and Rome failed to maintain their
national life for periods comparable to the long
endurance of those other peoples, was it not
just because the national system of ethics was
in each case undermined and fatally weakened
by the speculations of philosophers, who taught
effectively ethical doctrines incompatible with
the rigid conservatism of the old systems? Was
it not just for such teaching that Socrates was
condemned to drink the hemlock bowl? And,
if the old Roman religion and ethics owed their
decay less to the speculations of philosophers,

was not the downfall of the Roman civilization nevertheless due in the main to other influences of similar tendency? Of these influences, two seem to have been most powerful. First, Rome's success as a conquering power brought her into contact with, and into rulership over, so many peoples of diverse creeds and codes, and ultimately to the absorption of these multitudinous diverse elements within her system, that the old creed and the old ethico-political code, peculiar to and traditional to the small nucleus only of the vast Empire, were inevitably swallowed up and their power to guide the conduct of the Roman citizen fatally weakened. Secondly, the spread of Christianity within the Empire effected a radical transformation of the ethical system; or, rather, it substituted for the national system one essentially universal and non-political. These two processes of change favored each the other; and together they destroyed the ethical basis on which ancient Rome had founded and built up her political power. Rome, in short, attempted to assimilate, to Romanize, an immense mass of population of diverse races, creeds and codes; and in this attempt, her ethical system, the source of her power and the foundation of all her greatness, was destroyed.[1]

Systems of national ethics are, by their intrinsic nature, incapable of extension to alien peoples without losing their effectiveness to guide the lives of men. Hence those that have endured have done so only by remaining true to their intrinsic principles, by remaining strictly national and exclusive.

The universal systems and the peoples that have lived under their sway have had a very different history. These systems are by nature assimilative and missionary, seeking to extend themselves over all the world. The three great systems of this type have been so successful that they now include all peoples, save those few which had developed strong national systems before coming into contact and free rivalry with the universal codes. And in the main they have spread by destroying or supplanting

[1] In my "National Welfare and National Decay" I have accepted the view that a principal factor in the decline and fall of Rome was the deterioration of the population of the heart of the empire. This view (which, I note, has been substantially accepted by a great authority, Mr. W. E. Heitland, in his recently published "The Roman Fate") is not at variance with the statements made in the text; for the deterioration of the population and the decay of morals are two inseparable aspects of the one process of national degeneration.

the lesser national codes. Since their appearance, each initiated by a single great teacher, the history of the world has been essentially the history of the struggle between these universal systems and the multitude of national systems that had slowly developed during the long ages of the prehistoric period.

India, the original home of Buddhism, saw its rapid spread. For a time it must have seemed as though the universal ethics of Buddhism was destined to supplant the national Brahman code. But the latter, being bound up with and founded on caste, the most rigidly conservative of all systems, was already firmly set; it proved too strong to be displaced by the universal system. The latter faded from India and spread eastward among the peoples whose national systems were still small and primitive; and in China, where the national system was neither stimulated and hardened by caste nor tempered by war and by contact with other peoples, it was able to compromise with it and to spread by a process of infiltration. Its southward spread was checked by contact with one of its two great rivals, the more aggressive Moslem system. By this contact, Buddhism was thrown back from its southern outposts in the island world and confined to the continent.

The tendencies of a universal ethics are illustrated most clearly by the history of the Moslem world. The ethical system of Mohammed was planted by him among a people whose tribal creeds and cults were locally restricted and very primitive. It spread with astonishing rapidity, showing a tremendous power of assimilation. Peoples of the most diverse races — white, yellow, and black—and of the most diverse creeds and codes yielded before its onslaught and were welcomed within the fold; for it accepted all men without question, destroying race-prejudices and national sentiments. It abolished caste and ignored color, and broke down all barriers that divide man from man; and, what is more important and has been of greater effect in determining the history of the Moslem civilization, it broke down all the barriers that divide man from woman. The Arab mated freely with the Negro and with the yellow races, with the Malay, the Mongol and the Tartar.[1]

[1] In "The Future of Islam" Sir Wilfrid Blunt wrote: "It is there [Africa], indeed, that Islam has the best certainty of expansion and the fairest field for a propagation of its creed. Statistics, if they could be obtained, would, I am convinced, show an immense

The immensely rapid spread of the Moslem system was due no doubt, in part, to the simplicity of its code and to the relatively simple nature of its sanctions; for these enabled it to appeal effectively to all men. Its code was not too lofty for human attainment; its sanctions were not too remote and ethereal for effective appeal to common human nature. But, most of all, its success was due to the real equality it gave to all its converts. All were made equal in the eyes of God and man, and the career was opened to all the talents. Such multiplicity

---

Mohammedan progress within the last hundred years among the negro races, nor is this to be wondered at. Islam has so much to offer to the children of Man that it cannot fail to win them—so much more than any form of Christianity or European progress can give. The Christian missionary makes his way slowly in Africa. He has no true brotherhood to offer the negro except in another life. He makes no appeal to a present sense of dignity in the man he would convert. What Christian missionary takes a negress to wife or sits with the negro wholly as an equal at meat? Their relations remain at best those of teacher with taught, master with servant, grown man with child. The Mohammedan missionary from Morocco meanwhile stands on a different footing. He says to the negro, 'Come up and sit beside me. Give me your daughter and take mine. All who pronounce the formula of Islam are equal in this world and in the next.' In becoming a Mussulman even a slave acquires immediate dignity and the right to despise all men, whatever their color, who are not as himself. . . . Central Africa may then be counted on as the inheritance of Islam at no very distant day." Since this opinion and this forecaste were published, many other observers have found reason to accept and confirm them.

of contacts of diverse elements of race and culture, such manifold crossings and blendings of human stocks as were thus effected, could not fail to be immensely stimulating to human productivity. And so the rapid spread of the Moslem system was followed by the rise of a civilization astonishing both by the rate of its development and by the richness and variety of its achievements.

In a brief space of time Moslem learning, Moslem science and Moslem art became predominant on the earth; they covered a broad belt of the old world, from eastern Asia to Spain, with splendid mosques and libraries and universities; while all of Europe that lay beyond their influence still weltered in the chaos left by the breaking down of the Roman civilization.

But this rapid success was followed by a no less rapid decline. The destruction within the Moslem world of the old systems of national ethics rendered possible this rapid flourishing; but it removed at the same time their conserving stabilizing influences. Soon the brilliance of Moslem civilization was dimmed, a fatal inertia replaced its pristine vigor; and, though its religion still spreads among the more primitive peoples, worsting Christianity wherever they come into direct and fair competition as missionary powers, it has long ceased to add anything of note to the sum of human culture.

It has sometimes been assumed that the Moslem ethos is essentially opposed to progress in the higher things of the spirit. But, in the face of the great and rapid achievements of its early period, we can hardly accept that view. Rather, the history of Moslem civilization implies that a rapid development, soon to be followed by stagnation or actual decay, is its intrinsic tendency. And this twofold tendency, which its history so clearly displays, is inherent in its ethical system. The universal character of that system and of its religious sanctions, which led it to welcome all comers on equal terms, to override and ignore or destroy all barriers of race and nationality and caste, made for a multitude of stimulating contacts and set free the powers of all its converts from the constricting bands of local and narrow cults and of national or tribal codes.

But the Moslem ethos was lacking in conservative influence. And here we must distinguish widely between influences which are conservative and those which merely clog the wheels of progress and stifle the movements of the mind. Conservation is not the antagonist of progress and of liberalism; it is rather their proper and necessary complement, without which progress and liberalism lead only to early dissolution and decay. The essential expressions of conservatism are respect for the ancestors, pride in their achievement, and reverence for the traditions which they have handed down; all of which means what it is now fashionable to call "race-prejudice" and "national prejudice," but may more justly be described as preference for, and belief in the merits of, a man's own tribe, race, or nation, with its peculiar customs and institutions, its ethos in short. If such preferences, rooted in traditional sentiments, are swept away from a people, its component individuals become cosmopolitans; and a cosmopolitan is a man for whom all such preferences have become mere prejudices, a man in whom the traditional sentiments of his forefathers no longer flourish, a man who floats upon the current of life, the sport of his passions, though he may deceive himself with the fiction that he is guided in all things by reason alone.

Such a universal code breaks down also the

traditional groupings of mankind; it sets free each man from the control of the group-spirit, which, more than any other influence, renders men loyal members of society, ready to spend and sacrifice themselves for the good of the group, obedient to its laws and regardful of its future welfare.

In yet a third way, perhaps of greater effect than these other two, the Moslem ethos prepared the stagnation of its own culture. It happened that the Arab people, among whom the Moslem culture took its rise, inhabited a land which lay at the juncture of three continents, the historic homes of the three most distinctive races of mankind, the white, the yellow, and the black, and which was in touch also with the island homes of the Malay race. The breaking down of the barriers of national and racial exclusiveness led to the inter-marriage of Moslem converts of all these races. This may have contributed to accelerate the blooming of the Moslem culture, as it certainly contributed to accelerate the spreading of its influence. But the Arab founders freely mixed their blood with that of many other races and especially with that of the Negro race, a race

which never yet has shown itself capable of raising or maintaining itself unaided above a barbaric level of culture. It seems to me probable
in the highest degree that this miscegenation, and
especially perhaps the large infusion of Negro
blood into the peoples bearing the Moslem
culture, was a principal factor in bringing about
the rapid decline of that civilization. [1]

Now let us consider, from this point of view,
the history of the European peoples who became the heirs of the Græco-Roman civilization. We have noted how the national ethics of
Greece and of Rome were sapped and were sup-

[1] The Arabs are not devoid of pride of ancestry. Perhaps no
people has attached so much importance to descent in the male
line or kept so faithfully the records of such descent. Mohammed
is believed to have bequeathed his mantle to members of his own
tribe, the Koreysh, and to have said: "As long as there remains
one man of the Koreysh, so long shall that man be my successor"
and also to have declared: "If the Arab race falls, Islam shall fail."
And the Arabs are said to look down upon the Turks as barbarians.
Yet, in spite of the high value attached to Arab ancestry in the male
line, they seem to have had little or no care for purity of race, and
no objection to mating with the women of other races. Probably
the legitimacy and common practice of polygamy and concubinage
have played a leading part in bringing about this anomalous combination, intense pride of race and careful record of descent in the male
line combined with indifference to racial purity. This combination
is found not only in Africa and Arabia, but in all the regions into
which the Arab influence and blood has spread, from Borneo to
Bokhara; and indeed traces of it may be found as far as Timbuktu
and Morocco, Cordova and Budapest.

planted by the universal ethics of Christianity. We have now to notice that the peoples of northern and western Europe who came into contact with, and in various degrees under the influence of, the decaying Roman power and the rising power of the Christian Ethics, were for the most part organized in strong tribes and rudimentary nations, having their own strong systems of national ethics. And, when these contacts took place, the Roman civilization was already on the wane: its ethical system was in transformation; the national system that had been the foundation of the civil and military power of Rome was already largely destroyed by a system essentially incompatible with, and adverse to, the continuance of that power. This disharmony within the Roman civilization rendered it incapable of dominating the European peoples in the complete way in which Moslem conquerors have dominated their converts. The new converts were only partially converted. They became Christians; but they retained in large measure their national codes and cults. The Englishman became a Christian convert; but he continued to be primarily an Englishman and only secondarily a Christian; and, where the dictates of the two systems conflicted, those of the national system generally prevailed. The same was true in greater or less degree of all these new bearers of the civilization of Europe. So there grew up the strange anomaly of Christian Europe, a society of nations all of which had accepted the religion of peace and brotherhood, with its universal ethics, yet which were constantly at war with one another.

In the age of the Crusades, these nations made a short-lived attempt to sink their national differences and to combine in the defense of the Cross against the Crescent, of Christendom against the Moslem world. The success of this attempt was very partial only; the participating nations soon fell again into hostile groups; by the persistent rivalry of the nations within Christendom, their national differences became accentuated and their national peculiarities confirmed. And, though for a time they all gave allegiance to the head of the Christian Church, this allegiance was never more than nominal; the Church never effected the unification of Europe by securing the undisputed sway of the Christian ethics. If such unification had been achieved, European culture, untroubled by the series of national wars that make and mar so much of the history of Europe, might have bloomed as rapidly and as brilliantly as the culture of the Moslem world: and, possibly, its decline would have been equally rapid.

But it was not to be; the national divisions continued, the various nations took more definite shape, each developing its national culture on an ethical basis that was an imperfect and uneasy compromise between the national system and the universal system of Christianity. And to the present day this state of affairs continues. The European nations are characterized by the conglomerate nature of their ethics, an imperfect blend of the national and the universal systems.

Nowhere has this duality of the ethical basis been more clearly displayed than in England. There the national system has in the main prevailed over the universal. The King of England was exalted to be the head of a peculiar Church, which separated itself in frank hostility from the universal Christian Church; thus the influence of the universal ethical code was subordinated to, and made the instrument and servant of, the national code. The highest

duty of the Christian Englishman was to serve
God by serving his king and country. And,
when he began to spread his influence over a
large part of the surface of the earth, he was
always an Englishman first and a Christian
secondarily. The heathen might rightly be
converted to his Christian creed; but, unlike
the Moslem conqueror, he never accepted his
converts as his equals, or regarded them as
members of one great community equal before
God; and he consistently disdained to mix his
blood with theirs in marriage.

In these respects the English are typical of
the more northern peoples of Europe. The
peoples of the South, the southern French, the
Spaniards, the Portuguese, and the South Italians, partly perhaps because they were more completely Romanized, partly owing to their racial
constitution, were more completely Christian-
ized; among them the national code was less resistant to the universal code: consequently, the
course of their history has run more nearly after
the pattern of the Moslem world.

In spite of these differences, it remains true
that all the nations of Europe have developed on
this twofold ethical basis, have developed ethical

codes in which are mixed the incompatible
precepts of the universal and of the national
ethics. This disharmony of their ethical bases
has had profound effects; it has brought certain
advantages as well as great disadvantages.
Among the advantages we may place first the
stimulus to thought and discussion that comes
from the conflict of the incompatible elements
of the dual code. Where the national ethics
holds undisputed sway, as in early Rome, men
have no occasion to question its precepts.
And where, as in the Buddhist or the Moslem
world, a universal code alone rules the conduct
of men, there also discussion of ethical principles
finds no occasion. But where, as in Athens in
its prime, in the later Roman world, and in
modern Europe, the two systems are current
in imperfect combination, there doubt, ques-
tioning, and interminable discussion of ethical
principles inevitably occupy men's minds, stimulating them to habits of sceptical enquiry, the
effects of which are carried far beyond the bounds
of strictly ethical speculation. The progress
of European thought and culture has been, no
doubt, largely due to this influence.

The imperfect combination of the two ethi-

cal systems has been favorable to the progress of European culture in another way. The
influence of the universal system has played a
great part in bringing about the diffusion of
men of European origin over the surface of
the globe. Missionaries of Christianity have
been, in nearly all cases, very active in the
opening of new territories to European colonization. The story of the efforts of the Jesuit
missionaries in Canada, Louisiana, South America, Asia and the Pacific, striking and heroic
as it is, reveals only a small part of this vast
influence in shaping the present phase of world-
history. The colonization of North America
was largely due to the conflict between the two
systems; for it was this conflict that drove
the Pilgrim Fathers to seek new homes across
the ocean. They were men in whom the conflict between the two systems became acute
and in whom the universal prevailed over the
national system. Thus the dual ethics played
a great part in bringing about those contacts
with strange lands and strange peoples which
have reacted so strongly upon the European
nations, feeding the appetite for further knowledge, for better means of communication, and

for all that was novel, and enriching European civilization with a thousand things and practices brought from the remotest parts of the earth.

In yet a third way the duality of the ethical basis was favorable to progress. While the universal system worked as a liberalizing influence that set men's thoughts and actions free from the bonds which a strictly national system maintains, the persistence beside it of the national systems was a conservative influence which rendered possible the growth of stable nations, each developing its own peculiar variety of institutions and culture, each entering into a stimulating rivalry with the others. Thus was produced that diversity of culture within the bounds of a common civilization which has been a main condition of European progress. If Christian Rome had been strong enough to assimilate completely the tribes and nations within and around the Christian Empire, and had made of Christendom a single great Empire based only on Christian ethics, it is probable that its civilization, though it would have bloomed more rapidly, would, like that of the Moslem world, equally rapidly have sunk into apathy and stagnation, if not into actual decay. For, like the Moslem world, it would have lacked the national codes which, while maintaining diversity of cultures, gave strength and stability to the nations as they developed, each acquiring its own peculiar ethos and political structure.

Against these advantages of the dual system, we must set off certain grave drawbacks. The penalty of progress is unrest and a discontent, which, whether we call it divine or merely distressing, contrasts strongly with the peace and whole-heartedness of the saint, whether Buddhist, Moslem or Christian, and is equally far from the unquestioning devotion of the Samurai warrior who, in single-hearted acceptance of his national ethics, goes cheerfully and unquestioningly to meet death in the service of his Emperor and country.

In the soul of the European, two voices have contended for mastery; two claimants for his undivided allegiance have struggled within him, the one proclaiming the duties of the universal Christian code, the other urging obligations of service to his city, his State, his king and country, his nation. And the wars and bloody persecutions which have figured so largely in the history of Europe have been in the main the outcome of the rivalry between the two ethical systems. [1]

[1] Friederick Naumann, a sincere Christian and an acknowledged leader of Christian thought, has vividly expressed this conflict of the Christian soul in the following passage: "It is impossible to attempt to erect the entire development of mankind upon compassion and fraternal disposition. . . . This Gospel of the poor is one of the standards of our life, but not the only standard. Not our entire morality is rooted in the Gospel, but only a part of it, although an extremely important and easily despised constituent. Beside the Gospel there are demands of power and of right, without which society cannot exist. I myself do not know how to help myself in the conflict between Christianity and other tasks of life, save by the attempt to recognize the limits of Christianity. That is difficult, but it is better than the oppression of half-truths which I have had to bear. . . . Primitive Christianity attached no value to the preservation of the State, Law, Organization, Production. It simply does not reflect on the conditions of human society. This is in no sense a reproach, it is nothing but the determination of a limit: there exist human problems, of the greatest size and greatest difficulty, which are not essentially touched by the New Testament. By the occasional assurance of obedience towards the Roman Emperor, the question, as to how Christianity stands towards the State, is in no way solved. The State requires rulers, the democratic State as well as the aristocratic. . . . The State can, when it perfects itself, be impregnated with the motives of brotherly love, at least one can attempt it; but according to its nature, the State is not love, but constraint. The State does not belong to the sphere where, if a man takes away my coat, I am to let him have my cloak also; nor to that where sins are forgiven as soon as they are repented of. The State has no right to reckon with the end of the world, nor even with the voluntary goodness of all men. It forms part of the struggle for existence . . . a compound of human wills, of soldiers, of paragraphs and oppressions. This compound is, in all its harshness, the prerequisite of culture. And it found its pattern form in Rome, not in Nazareth. . . . We possess a knowl-

The persecution of the Christians in the Roman Empire was the first phase. There the national spirit was dominant; the Christians were persecuted, not because they held certain religious beliefs, but because, inspired by the universal ethics of Christianity, they refused to acknowledge the claim upon their allegiance made by the ethics of the Roman State.

---

edge of the world, which teaches us a God of power and strength, who sends out life and death, as simultaneously as shadow and light, and a revelation, a faith as to salvation, which declares the same God to be Father. The following of the world-God produces the morality of the struggle for existence, and the service of the Father of Jesus Christ produces the morality of compassion. And yet, they are not two Gods, but one God. Somehow or other their arms intertwine. Only, no mortal can say, where and how this occurs. That is indeed a pain, and religion without pain does not exist, has never existed. . . . Military power is the foundation of all order in the State and of all prosperity in the society of Europe. Say all that you know against the military! It will all be correct; for the description of battles cannot be more awful than the reality. And then go with me to where military power existed in the past, and where it now exists no longer—to the countries by the Mediterranean. The man who does not see what the collapse of the Roman military government involved is beyond cure. All the evils of military power are slight compared with the misery of a country in which no such rule exists. Dearth of soldiery means, in reality, ruins, decline, beggary, and war of all against all.

An armed peace is not beautiful, but it is better than all past conditions known to us through history. All our culture would go the way of the Arabian culture, were we to grow weak in a military sense. . . . Hence, we either dare to aim at being without a State, and thus throw ourselves deliberately into the arms of anarchy; or we decide to possess, alongside of our religious creed, a political creed as well." (" *Briefe über Religion.*")

With the conversion of the Roman world to Christianity, the two systems of ethics came into open conflict or hardly disguised rivalry in all parts of the empire. The universal system rapidly gained the upper hand. The Church, asserting its claim to be the supreme temporal power, effected a partial synthesis and co-operation of the universal and the national systems of ethics; and, supporting its claim with the tremendous sanctions of the Christian religion, it dominated Europe for more than a thousand years. During this period it suppressed the manifestations of the spirit of nationality, and achieved in large measure a unity of Christendom in which national distinctions seemed in a fair way to disappear.[1] But the spirit of nationality and the

[1] "In consequence of this opposition between the Church and the World, patriotism and the sense of civic duty, the most elevated and splendid of all social sentiments in the pre-Christian civilization of the Greco-Roman world, tended, under the influence of Christianity, either to expand into universal philanthropy, or to be concentrated on the ecclesiastical community. 'We recognize one commonwealth, the World,' says Tertullian; 'We know,' says Origen, 'that we have a fatherland founded by the word of God.'" (H. Sidgwick, *History of Ethics*, p. 120.) The difference between the Ethics of early Christianity and the national Ethics of Greece and Rome appears in nothing more clearly than in their estimations of the functions of parenthood. While by the latter (as by all other systems of National Ethics) these functions were regarded as sacred duties; by the former

old national systems were not dead, though slumbering; and, as the spirit of enquiry began to move again in Europe, men's minds attained to a greater independence, became less subject to the influence of the awful sanctions wielded by the Church. Then the national systems began to assert themselves again, and a tremendous conflict began. The so-called wars of religion were incidents of the resistance offered by the national systems to complete absorption and destruction, of the endeavor to check and throw off the increasing dominance of the Church of Rome.

A contemporary historian has summarized the story in the following passage: "In a futile attempt to arrest the decay of religious assendancy, the Papacy had sanctioned a system of persecution of the heretical adherents of the Reformation, more terrible than that suffered by the early Christians at the hands of the Romans. In the ferocity of the methods used, and in the number of victims resulting

---

they were deprecated as mere consequences of the fact that marriage is the smaller of two evils, that it is better to marry than to burn. This radical change of view had been to some extent prepared by the teaching of the Stoic philosophers, the more extreme of whom had taught a universal Ethics, and by the asceticism of the Neo-Platonists.

therefrom, it far distanced its earlier prototype. For a century and a half Europe was racked by internecine religious wars and persecutions, which spared no man, no land. Throughout the 17th century these convulsions continued. Civil wars in England, the Thirty Years' War in Germany, the Dragonnades in France, the Inquisition in Portugal and Spain, the massacres in Holland—all had as their apparent motive the suppression of Protestant heresy. In reality they were phases of a bloody struggle for the supremacy of a new ideology. The latent forces of politics had pushed upward. Politics was about to supplant religion as the motive force of social life, and Politics prevailed. Politics left as much of the religious doctrine intact as did not interfere with its fundamental requirement of allegiance. The Church remained, but it became in theory the subservient tool of the State." [1]

What Mr. Wallace has here called 'politics' was the spirit, the ethics, of nationality; and what he calls 'religion' was the universal ethics of Christianity. The bloody conflict he describes was not, as he asserts, a struggle between

[1] W. K. Wallace, "The Trend of History," p. 8, N. Y., 1922.

religion and politics. For the sanctions of religion were invoked on both sides. It was a new phase of the struggle between the two ethical systems. And, in the struggle, the spirit of nationality, in order to meet on equal terms its great rival, in order to support its claims with religious sanctions no less strong than those of the Roman Church, devised and adopted the theory of the divine right of kings; for at that time kings were the symbols of the spirit of nationality. Thus the Reformation was essentially political and ethical rather than religious. It was the triumphant rejection by several of the national systems of the claim to dominance made by the Roman Church in the name of universal ethics.

The spirit of nationality, whose victory in the Reformation ushered in the modern period of European history, has continued to prevail more and more throughout Europe up to the present day; and, more than any other factor, it has shaped the history of the modern world.

The Great War was the culmination of this modern tendency. It was provoked by a nation in which the universal ethics had become completely subordinated to the ethics of nationality, in which the influence of Christian ethics had fallen so low that it failed to restrain and mitigate the boundless aspirations of an unbridled nationalism.

And the Great War has brought no solution of the problem, but rather has accentuated it everywhere. Everywhere, in private conduct and in national policy, we are confronted by the perplexities arising from our dual system of ethics, from the conflict between the claims of nationality and citizenship on the one hand and of the brotherhood of man upon the other.

This unresolved conflict is the essential ground of the present intolerable situation in Europe. France stands out as the embodiment of the spirit of nationality; and most of those who deprecate and condemn her present action are moved in some degree by the spirit of universal ethics. The perplexities of individuals arising from the same source are no less great than the perplexities of nations. The position of the conscientious objector during the Great War was but the clearest illustration of such personal perplexities and dilemmas.

The Boer War, waged by England at the close of the 19th century, illustrated the same truth even more vividly. For, in that war, the British nation was acutely and almost evenly divided between those who gave precedence to the national system and those whose opinion was molded by the universal ethics of Christianity.

LECTURE II

Our Need of Some Synthesis of the Two Systems

If we turn now to enquire—What has been the influence of the speculations of moral philosophers upon the ethical basis of European civilization during the Christian era?—we see that, with few exceptions, they have thrown their influence on the side of the universal code. This has been true, not only of the great Christian moralists, but also of those who were not specifically Christian. The formula of Kant— "Treat no man as a means, but every man as an end in himself"; the formula of Bentham and the Utilitarians—"Act for the greatest good of the greatest number"; the formula of Schopenhauer, which acknowledges acts of loving kindness as the whole sum of moral action,—all these are clearly universalist formulas. They take no account of the great fact of nationality;

they ignore the obligations and duties that arise therefrom; they are formulas fitted only for a world that has passed beyond the need for civil government, for national defense, for patriotic self-sacrifice, for loyalty to fellow citizens or fellow tribes-men, and to national or tribal institutions. It is true that a few thinkers, notably Machiavelli, Bodin, and Hobbes, have sought to justify and establish the principle of nationality. But they were regarded as political rather than as ethical philosophers; for the world had forgotten the lesson taught by Plato, that the principles of ethics and of politics are inseparable.

The modern world has produced one striking exception to the rule that the moral philosophers have thrown their influence on the side of the universal code, namely, the ethical system of which the philosopher Hegel was the great exponent. Here we have an ethical system propounded by philosophers which threw its whole weight against the universal ethics and on the side of the ethics of nationalism. It was essentially a worship of the State as the highest expression in our world of the Universal Mind or Reason. It taught that the State was that for the sake of which men exist; that each man is before all things a citizen; and that all his ethical obligations derive from his status as a citizen, a member of a larger whole apart from which he is of no value and has no ethical rights or duties. According to the teachings of this system, a man's conduct is right or moral in so far as he obeys the State, serves it, promotes its welfare, plays a part as a faithful cog in the great machine; but, in so far as his acts may have no relation to the welfare of this larger whole, they are morally indifferent, without ethical significance. The Kantian doctrine is reversed; each man is no longer an end in himself, but solely a means to an end, namely the welfare of the State. This moral philosophy, being a revival and extreme development of the nationalist system of ethics[1] was eagerly accepted by the Prussian State, in which it took shape: and this State, having elaborated a very

[1] It was also a perversion of the national ethics, in so far as the State was regarded by it, not as identical with the nation, nor as the nation viewed in one of its several aspects, nor as the instrument of the nation, but as a metaphysical entity superior to and presiding over the people whose only duty was to obey and serve it. This was the earlier form of this philosophy of the State. Later exponents, notably Treitschke, identified the State with the nation: and the British Hegelians have done much to purge the system of this perverse and inhuman feature.

efficient system of public instruction, assiduously propagated this code so acceptable to its ambitions; until, after little more than half a century, the national ethics preponderated greatly in influence over the universal system.

We have witnessed and Europe has suffered the terrible effects that may be produced in the modern world by a system of strictly National Ethics, unsoftened, unrestrained by an admixture of Universal Ethics. The nation thus prompted and thus unrestrained broke loose like a wild beast within the community of Christian nations, slaughtering and destroying with a ruthlessness that shocked the rest of the western world and provoked it to combine in moral censure and armed resistance.

This episode of recent history has brought to the front, in public discussion and in private reflection, the great ethical problem that confronts the modern world. It has made obvious to all men the fact that the most urgent need of the present age is an adequate ethical system. It has shown that our civilization can no longer endure upon the dual ethical basis, an ethical hodge-podge of elements mixed from two conflicting and unreconciled systems. The conscience

of mankind is profoundly disturbed. Western
civilization is sick; its condition is similar to
that of the neurotic patient who is torn by
conflicting and irreconcilable] desires; its moral
energies are wastefully consumed by the internal
conflict, instead of being devoted to profitable
work that would carry our civilization onward
to higher levels. The patient suffers from aboulia
or lack of will power, from various anesthesias
and amnesias, from paralysis, from bad dreams
of calamities to come, and from a vague but
acute distress. He sees no way of escape, no way
in which his conflict may be resolved and his
energies once more directed, in harmonious
co-operation, towards some clearly envisaged
goal. Just as the neurotic patient can be cured
only by a complete readjustment of his moral
basis, by frankly facing and analyzing his
problem, by going down to his moral foundations and laying them anew; so also our civilization can be cured, not by any tinkering with
symptoms, by moral exhortation, or by sporadic
acts of charity to starving peoples, on however
great a scale, but only by facing our moral
problem, diagnosing its true nature, and thinking out a real solution of it.

The natural unthinking reaction of the earnest
Christian or of any man of humane sentiments,
in face of the distracted and deeply troubled
world, is to denounce the ethics of nationalism
as accursed, and to demand that it be wholly
swept away to give immediate and undisputed
sway to the universal ethics of Christianity.
Such a man is apt to assert that, if only all men
and all nations would follow strictly the precepts of the Sermon on the Mount, all would
be well with the world. And, misled by the
narrow teachings of the greater number of
the moral philosophers who, ignoring the claims
of national ethics, have taught almost exclusively the principles of universal individualist ethics, the greater part of civilized mankind
has learnt to regard the universal system as
alone ethical or moral, and, while yet practising
in various ways the principles of national
ethics, never realizes that these also are moral
principles that have their valid claim upon our
allegiance.

The civilized man of to-day gives a theoretical
allegiance to the universal system only; but, when
the two systems conflict, he follows in the main
the principles of national ethics, justifying such

practices, if he at all seeks to justify them, on the ground of urgent practical necessity. And so he repeatedly and constantly finds his practice inconsistent with his professed and consciously accepted ethical principles. And, in the practice of the national ethics under the plea of practical necessity, he lacks the guidance of any mature reflection upon the ethical problems involved. Further, in the advocacy and execution of all national policies, he finds himself hampered, not only by the lack of such deliberately reasoned principles, but also by the fact that such policies are perpetually attacked and opposed by all those who, claiming to speak in the name of morality, urge against such policies the precepts of universal ethics, the only ethics officially recognized and taught as such among us.

Thus the citizen of any one of our modern nations finds himself involved in a situation which is both perplexing and demoralizing. He finds himself supporting national policies which are widely denounced as immoral and which are unmistakably opposed to the generally recognized principles of universal ethics. Yet his good sense forbids him to abandon or to oppose these policies; though he cannot reconcile them with his ethical principles, the only ethical principles that he has been taught to recognize as such.

The earnest Christian who finds himself supporting his nation in war and perhaps shouldering a rifle in the ranks illustrates most strikingly this perplexity of the modern mind and this discrepancy between men's practice and their acknowledged ethical principles.

Let me point to some other similar perplexities which confront more especially the citizen of the United States of America. Shall America join the League of Nations? Universal Ethics bids him with no uncertain voice join the League without hesitation or reservation. But National Ethics says 'No'; and in the main he obeys the latter, with an uneasy sense that, though he is acting wisely and patriotically, he is acting wrongly.

Again, hordes of semi-destitute people from Southern Europe and the Near East are clamoring for admission to the United States. Universal Ethics says unmistakably that they must be freely admitted; that the American citizen has no right to claim as his alone the immense economic resources of his land; that he must be

prepared to share them equally with all comers;
and that, the more numerous and ignorant and
poverty-stricken and barbarous these claimants
may be, the stronger is their claim to share in the
economic and cultural advantages which he so
copiously enjoys. Yet, in the main, the American
citizen agrees to put up the bars and to narrow
the gates, feeling that he is compelled by good
sense to do what his ethical principles forbid.

A very similar problem confronts him on his
western coast. The good sense of the inhabitants
of California and of the other western coast-
states prompts them strictly to forbid the entry
and naturalization of any further thousands of
the natives of Asia; and, while their eastern
critics condemn them in the name of universal
ethics, they stoutly maintain their position;
though they may not know how to justify it in
the court of ethics, and cannot but feel uneasy
and perplexed at finding themselves steadily
set upon a course of action inconsistent with
their own accepted moral principles.

Another illustration: the principles of universal ethics and their northern exponents in this
country demand that the American Negro shall
be given social and political equality; yet, though

for sixty years the Federal law, determined by these principles and these exponents, has prescribed such equality, the good sense of the Southern white man still steadily forbids him to obey these precepts and impels him in a course of conduct inconsistent with his acknowledged ethical principles.

I need hardly point out that the Englishman is confronted by similar perplexities of equal gravity and greater number. There is no citizen of the countries comprised under Western Civilization that is exempt from similar moral difficulties.

Yet one last illustration, which is perhaps more likely than the others I have cited to appeal directly to the academic mind. The principles of universal ethics demand that all citizens of this country shall enjoy equal opportunities and equal advantages of education. To go through the college and university, continuing academic studies up to the age of twenty-two or even twenty-five years, has undoubtedly proved to be a great advantage and opportunity to many of those who have taken such courses of prolonged study. It follows from the principles of universal ethics that the country must accept, as its settled ideal and practical policy, the putting of every boy and girl through a college and university course. And this ideal, which results with logical necessity from the universal principles, is already widely proclaimed, and some steps have been made towards its realization.[1] Yet, although this program is hitherto in practice on a very small scale only, we hear already on every hand the voice of good sense protesting against it, in the light of the experience gained in the last few years. Almost every day the attentive observer may note that some experienced educator raises his voice in protest. We are told broadly that too many people are going to college; that the universities are seriously overcrowded; that the machinery of higher education cannot cope with the flood; that university education is giving place to a quasi-mechanical process of instruction which bears an uncanny likeness to the process of fattening fowls by machinery. Or, more enlighteningly, we are told that a large proportion of the young people who are even now crowding the universities are

[1] A similar claim is now finding voice within the labor party in England. The claim includes, not only free access to all universities, but also entire material support of all university students by the State.

not fitted to profit by university education, that they are not of the intellectual and moral calibre that must be presupposed in its clientele by any true university system.

Why, then, cannot we escape from our perplexities by courageously putting into practice the officially and generally accepted principles of universal ethics?[1]

The answer in brief is that the good sense which, in all the foregoing and in many other instances, finds itself opposed to the precepts of universal ethics is not, as so commonly alleged, the expression of mere selfishness and immorality. It is rather the expression of the rival ethics, the system of National Ethics, which, though now unformulated and unacknowledged by our moral philosophers, has nevertheless played an essen-

[1] These principles may be defined concisely as the practice of a universal and strictly impartial philanthropy. The demands of such philanthropy are well stated by Prof. R. B. Perry in the following passage: "Though there may be no express hostility to the more developed cultural activities, nevertheless the motive of philanthropy is to bring up those who have fallen behind, *even if it be necessary to halt the vanguard* of human attainment. So long as there is a single human being starving, every other consideration is to be subordinated to getting that man fed [and, it might fairly be added, well clothed and educated]. It will be time to think of perfection—such is the feeling of the philanthropist—when those who are in deadly peril have been brought to a place of safety." ("The Present Conflict of Ideals.")

tial part in the progress of civilization and still
has a very essential part to play in the future;
which in fact is required now, as never before in the
history of the world, to exert a conservative influence, mitigating and correcting the principles
of Universal Ethics.

This brief answer needs to be developed at
some length. The verdicts of common sense or
good sense, which, in the instances I have
mentioned and in so many others, are directly
opposed to the precepts of universal ethics,
need to be philosophically justified and defended
against the host of critics who claim to speak
in the name of morality. For, so long as the
champions of good sense are plausibly represented as striving for immoral ends or as using
immoral means, their hands are weakened, their
resolution is apt to be sicklied o'er with the pale
cast of doubt, and their cause is in danger of
defeat.

What I have to say is, then, in the first place
a defense of some of these verdicts of good sense
and an attempt to show that they are the verdicts
of the neglected national ethics; secondly, the
demonstration that national ethics is a necessary
moral complement of the universal ethics of

Christianity; thirdly, an attempt to harmonize, reconcile, or synthesize in some degree the principles of the two systems of ethics, which hitherto have remained in open conflict.

Let us go back to the question of the humane man and the sincere Christian, who says—Why not solve our perplexities by boldly and strictly following the precepts of Christian Ethics, applying them to the solution, not only of our private personal problems, but also to all public and political problems?

This demand, when it is translated into terms of political action, takes two principal alternative forms. And I do not know of any other form under which it could take political expression. The one form is the ideal of the philosophic anarchists, of Tolstoi, of Kropotkin, and their fellows; the ideal of a world that should need no government, because every man and woman would obey with perfect self-suppression and perfect wisdom the dictates of the universal ethics of human brotherhood. No doubt, if this revolution could be brought about, the state of the world would be improved. But the experience of nearly two thousand years shows that this demand and this hope cannot be fulfilled.

They could be fulfilled only if human nature could be radically transformed, in a manner and degree that we know to be impossible. Human nature, the constitution which each of us inherits, the innate endowment of the species *Homo Sapiens*, is the product of a long slow process of evolution; this native basis can be changed only very slowly.

Our innate constitution is not, as John Locke said, and as the optimistic philosophers of the nineteenth century believed, a *tabula rasa*, a clean wax tablet, plastic to receive and to retain whatever form and impress may be given to it. If this doctrine were true, it would follow that we need only to improve the environment in order to transform the whole human race into perfect beings. This was the false philosophy upon which the hopes and the practices of the philanthropists of the nineteenth century were mainly founded.

Human nature, the innate constitution of the species, may more truly be likened to a palimpsest, a tablet that bears the deep and ineradicable impressions of the experience of the race, impressions made during the millions of years in which the race struggled slowly and painfully upward from the intellectual and moral levels of our animal ancestry.[1]

The mass of mankind cannot be made into angels in the course of a few years, nor in the course of a few generations, by any natural process. We must cut our coat according to our cloth; we must seek to develop such an ethical and political system as will effectively harmonize for social ends those energies of human nature that are common to the whole race of man, those ancient instinctive energies that are the very foundation of our being, the springs of all our activities. In short, the ideal of the Christian or philosophic anarchist, of Tolstoi or Kropotkin, the ideal that would do away with all government and all political institutions is, we know, an impossible one. Men need to be governed, need to be members of an organized polity, if they are to realize the best potentialities of their nature. Only by partaking in the life

[1] I am aware, of course, that at the present time a school of reactionary psychologists in this country is trying to persuade us that Locke's old doctrine of the *tabula rasa* is true. I cannot here set forth the overwhelming weight of evidence against this view. Nor need I refer you to my own published discussions of this topic. It suffices to appeal against this academic freak doctrine to the good sense and universal experience of mankind. The doctrine is a product of the cloistered academic mind, and, in its contemporary form, of minds cloistered in psychological laboratories.

of an organized political community, held together by ancient firmly-rooted traditions, ethical and political, has man risen from savagery; and only by further development and improvement of his ethical traditions and political institutions can he hope to rise above the very modest level he has so far attained.[1]

A large part of mankind does live under the sway of the universal ethics of Buddhism; and though in some regions, as in China and Thibet, this universal system does not reign alone, but, as with Christian ethics in Europe, is modified by some infusion of national ethics, there are regions in which such modification is but slight; there we may observe the influence of the universal system as exercised in relative purity. Such a region is Burma. And we may fairly turn to Burma to learn what consequences may be expected from such undisputed sway of universal ethics. What then is the spectacle presented by the people of Burma? In many respects it is attractive. It has been asserted that the Burmese are the happiest people in the world. They are mild-mannered and gentle, mutually tolerant

[1] The reader to whom this truth is not a truism may find a reasoned exposition of it in "The Group Mind."

and forbearing, and singularly free from the more violent vices and crimes, as befits the followers of Buddha. But, against this, we have to set off their indolence and their intellectual sloth, which have kept the whole people in a condition of stagnation, preventing the development of their civilization beyond a rudimentary level in the spheres of art and literature, and forbidding even the rudiments of scientific culture; so that gross superstition abounds, and the people remains without power to protect itself against the major accidents of nature and the hostility of other peoples. Contemplating such a people we may well be tempted to exclaim with the poet—"Better fifty years of Europe than a cycle of Cathay!"

The second prescription, widely advocated and less remote, perhaps, from the realities of life than the anarchic ideal, is that of a Cosmopolitan government, under whose mild rule all national frontiers and national governments should be swept away and mankind should settle down as one happy family to live peacefully for evermore.

By a strange confusion of thought, this ideal is often spoken of and advocated as Internationalism. This implies, I say, a strange and puerile confusion of thought, a gross failure to distinguish between two very different systems or ideals, the Cosmopolitan and the International ideals. For surely it needs no deep reflection to discern the difference between these two ideals. There can be no Internationalism, that is, no settled regime of friendly rivalry and considerate dealing between nations, when all national boundaries shall have been swept away, when nations shall have been abolished and national governments shall have abdicated in favor of one universal parliament of mankind.

This ideal of a Cosmopolitan government, superseding the functions of national governments and embracing in one great nation all the peoples of the world, is perhaps, unlike the anarchic ideal, not impossible of realization. It even seems possible that, if Germany had achieved the success towards which she came so near in the late war, if, let us say, Marshal Foch had died of measles when a child or had been killed by a stray shell in the early stages of the war, then the cosmopolitan system might have been established and might be even now in pretty good running-order.

But, though it may be a possible system, we have to face the question—Is it a desirable system? Would mankind flourish under any such system, bringing forth the highest and finest fruits of human endeavor?

I have attempted to give a reasoned answer to that question in my "Group Mind." And I may repeat here very concisely the conclusion to which that investigation led me. The answer is No—mankind could not continue to flourish and progress under such a cosmopolitan system. In spite of all the drawbacks and dangers inevitably involved in the existence of nations and the flourishing of the spirit of nationality, drawbacks and dangers that are obvious to the meanest intelligence, nations are necessary institutions; for the following reasons:

1. Man is a social being; he cannot live and thrive alone; and he can be induced to work consistently for the good of his fellow-men, and in harmonious coöperation with them, only by participation in the life of an enduring organized group, a group that has a long history in which he may take pride and an indefinitely long future on which he may fix his larger hopes. Identification of the individual with such a

group is the only way in which the mass of mankind can be brought to live consistently on a plane of altruistic effort and public-spirited endeavor, observing high standards of social conduct such as must be accepted and must prevail in any community, if it is to flourish on a high plane, if it is to maintain and develop a culture worthy in any sense to be called civilization.

2. Only a group that is completely individualized and self-contained can effectively subdue and turn to the higher uses of social life the egoistic impulses of men in general. Only such a group can find a place and a function for the talents and ambitions of every man who is born into it, making each individual a member of its vital organization; only such a group can give scope and effective stimulus to all the potentialities of each of its members. Any group less than the nation, any such group as a professional or trade association, or a league of socialists or reformers of any kind, even if it be world-wide in its scope, is incapable of doing for its members what the nation can and in various degrees does do for its citizens, in the way of raising their lives above the animal plane of self-seeking or of merely family altruism.

3. The universal, world-wide, or cosmopolitan State cannot replace the nations in the performance of these elevating functions of nationality, for two good reasons. First, such a cosmopolitan group would be too vast and too heterogeneous to call effectively into play the social potentialities of men in general; men cannot effectively conceive so vast a group, cannot envisage its needs, cannot trace in imagination the effects upon its life of their own efforts and their own sacrifices; they cannot sympathetically share the desires and emotions, the joys and sorrows, of so vast a multitude, most of whom live under conditions which they cannot even remotely imagine, have needs which they cannot understand, and aspirations which they cannot share.

Secondly, even if all this were possible, there would remain a different and equally fatal weakness inherent in the cosmopolitan system. Just as individuals need the stimulus of example, of emulation, and of contact with a variety of types, if their highest powers are to be evoked, so nations and all other groups require similar stimulus; they need the appeal of emulation to evoke their best efforts. And civilization as a whole requires, if it is to progress, the variety of

social and political experiment, the varied special-
izations of collective function and effort, which can
be provided only by the rivalry of a number of
nations, each developing, under its own peculiar
conditions and in accordance with its peculiar
racial genius, its own unique historical process.

In addition to these inherent weaknesses, any
cosmopolitan system that might replace the
nations, if it were organized upon any principle
that could claim to be democratic in any appre-
ciable sense or degree, would suffer a fatal weakness from its mere size. We know now, from the
experience of the last century, how great are the
difficulties of representative democracy, even
when adopted as the working politics of the most
stable and experienced nations; how difficult it
is to secure any effective voice to minorities;
how easily abuses and distortions of the political
process arise, and how difficult it is to rectify
them when once they have become established.
All these difficulties would be magnified immensely under the cosmopolitan system. Such
a system could be maintained only as an autocracy; and that, as we know, would offer not the
feeblest guarantees, not the faintest prospect,
of continued and harmonious development.

The foregoing paragraphs are a highly condensed statement of the argument for Nationalism, and for the sentiment of patriotism or national loyalty, as essential conditions of the good life for the masses of mankind. It is fashionable, among those intellectuals who claim for themselves a monopoly of enlightened liberalism and humane sentiment, to decry patriotism as a barbarous survival which, whatever excuse or justification it may have had in the past, can now and in the future work only harm to mankind. This belittling of patriotism is one of the stock features of the repertoire of the Cosmopolitan in his attacks upon Nationalism. But the more the influence of religion wanes, the more urgently and obviously do we need the influences of enlightened patriotism and of group loyalties of every sort.

If one had to attempt to compare religion with patriotism as influences making for morality throughout the history of mankind, I, for one, should not hesitate to give patriotism the higher place. Fortunately, throughout the development of European civilization, with its dual system of ethics, the dominance of sentiment over logic, so natural to the mass of mankind, has permitted these two great sources of moral effort, religion and patriotism, to coöperate in large measure, in spite of the logical incompatibility of patriotism with the universal ethics.

In order to realize the immensely beneficial influence of patriotism in this *mélange* of religion and patriotism, we have only to turn to the history of a country saturated with religion but devoid of patriotism. Such a country (I speak of the past, not of the present and very recent past) is India. Let us hear what a great critic has to say of this matter. Mr. William Archer, pondering the problems of India's future in the light of its past, writes as follows, in a book which has never been surpassed, I think never equalled, for clarity of vision and humane wisdom on this baffling topic: "It is not through religion alone that morality can be raised to the temperature at which it passes into our blood and nerve—into the very fibre of our being. All that is needed is to kindle a sentiment . . . of loyalty to something higher than our own personal or family interests —'something, not ourselves, that makes for' or rather demands, 'righteousness.'"[1] He then writes of "patriotism as an inspiring principle"

[1] "India and the Future."

as follows: "Where are we to find in India this 'something not ourselves'? To appeal to the Indian masses on the ground of world-citizenship—of their participation in the onward march of humanity—would be so premature that the suggestion sounds ironic. But may not the necessary stimulus be found in that very idea of India, of the Motherland, which a timorous or merely selfish policy would have us proscribe as seditious? . . . the loyalty of the Indian schoolboy of the near future should be encouraged to attach itself, not merely to his caste or sect, but to his country. Whether we like it or not, this is what will happen—nay, is happening in certain parts of India. It seems to me that the only true wisdom for the Government is to recognize that the inevitable is also the desirable, and to seek in patriotism that reinforcement of character which is falsely declared to be the peculiar property of religion. 'Bande Mataram' should no longer be the watchword of sedition, but should be accepted as the inspiring principle of a great effort of national regeneration. It should be the motto, not only of the schoolroom, but of the secretariat."

These are wise words. India illustrates most

forcibly the fact that, where nationalism does
not exist, or is but feeble, it is necessary to
develop it, in order to render a people capable of
self-government, to inspire in them the spirit of
public service, of devotion to a community
wider than the family. The difference between
the recent histories of Japan and China has been
in the main determined by the fact that the
sentiment of patriotism has long been cultivated
in Japan much more effectively than in China.
In consequence, while the one people seems to be
on the road which will lead it to the highest place
among the nations, as a leader in civilization and
international morality, the other, remaining inert
and helpless in all dealings with the outer world
and a prey to civil war and to internal disorders
of all kinds, is threatened with universal decay.

Nationalism, then, is a great force, the greatest
force in the modern world; and, like other great
forces, it is capable of doing much good or much
harm, according as it is directed wisely or un-
wisely. Love of one's country, or patriotism,
does not necessarily involve or tend to generate
chauvinism, the hatred of other nations; though
the two utterly unlike sentiments are often con-
fused through lack of precision of thought and

language. It must be admitted also that much of current nationalism is rooted in chauvinism as well as in patriotism. When humanitarians, cosmopolitans, and anarchists denounce nationalism, they have in mind, no doubt, that kind of nationalism in which chauvinism plays a prominent part. But their crusade against nationalism is unwise, not only because nationalism (founded in patriotism) is the greatest of forces capable of elevating the masses of mankind, but also because, as all history shows, no such crusade has the faintest prospect of success. In the face of this tremendous and world-wide moral force, it is the part of wisdom, not to attempt to oppose or to eradicate it, but to guide it to noble ends, and to purify, with sympathetic understanding, the sentiment of patriotism which should be, and is, its main root and stem.[1]

---

[1] George Eliot, with that wonderful wisdom which repeatedly evokes our admiration, stated the essence of this matter in the following lines:

"An individual man, to be harmoniously great, must belong to a nation . . . A common humanity is not yet enough to feed the rich blood of various activity which makes a complete man. The time is not come for cosmopolitanism to be highly virtuous, any more than for communism to suffice for social energy. I am not bound to feel for a Chinaman as I feel for my fellow-countryman: I am bound not to demoralize him with opium, not to compel him to my will by destroying or plundering the fruits of his labors on the alleged ground that he is not cosmopolitan enough, and not

A system of universal ethics, expressing itself either as a universal anarchy or as a single cosmopolitan world-embracing State, is then not a tenable ideal, not an ideal that can reasonably be made the goal of our endeavor. For, as we have seen, it would, if it were realized under either form, fail to develop or maintain a civilization under which human nature would flourish and put forth its best fruits, realize its potentialities to the full. Under either form, civilization would stagnate; because men would lack the conditions essential to the realization of their highest potentialities, both moral and intellectual.

It may be added that, not only would either system prove very unsatisfactory, if it could be established, because unsuited to bring out the best that is in human nature, but also human

---

to insult him for his want of my tailoring and religion, when he appears as a peaceable visitor on the London pavement. It is admirable in a Briton with a good purpose to learn Chinese, but it would not be a proof of fine intellect in him to taste Chinese poetry in the original more than he tastes the poetry of his own tongue. Affection, intelligence, duty, radiate from a centre, and nature has decided that for us English folk that centre can be neither China nor Peru. Most of us feel this unreflectingly; for the affectation of undervaluing everything native, and being too fine for one's own country, belongs only to a few minds of no dangerous leverage. What is wanting is, that we should recognize a corresponding attachment to nationality as legitimate in every other people, and understand that its absence is a privation of the greatest good."

nature is such as to offer immense, perhaps in-
superable, difficulties to the perpetuation of
any such system. Man is so constituted that he
inevitably develops attachments to those of his
fellows who are nearest to him, who most re-
semble him in their customs, their ways of thinking and feeling; with them he finds himself in
sympathy and strongly desires to be in sympathy.
He prefers their company to that of men less
like himself; he is prejudiced in their favor as
against all other men; he understands their
point of view, because he sympathizes with
them. In other words, men in general are incapable of that strict impartiality which the
universal ethics requires of them. It is only a
rare individual here and there who achieves a
truly universal or cosmopolitan attitude; and
he generally achieves his impartiality, not by
extending his warmer sympathies to all men, but
rather by withdrawing from all more intimate
relations and becoming equally indifferent to all
men, with great loss to his own moral nature
and development.

The immense force and wide spread of the
spirit of nationality in the modern world illustrate this fundamental trait of human nature.

For its rise has coincided with the great improvements in means of communication which have multiplied a thousand-fold the contacts between men of different races and nations. And this multiplication of contacts, instead of destroying or weakening the barriers of nationality, the "prejudices" of race, the partiality of men for their own kind, has but accentuated these things, fostered their growth, intensified their influences throughout the world; until now these national partialities, these national prejudices and preferences rooted in national sentiments, have become the most powerful political forces of the modern world and, more than any other factors, more even than the immense economic forces of the industrial age, have shaped the history of the Western world throughout the last century. The operation of these "irrational" forces has falsified again and again the economic interpretation of history, and is accountable for the fact that the prophecies of the economists have generally been so wide of the mark.[1] Against these "irra-

---

[1] The prophecies of economists made before the Great War in respect to the possibilities of European war are only the most striking illustration of the fact, among many others. It was generally asserted by them that a European war was fast becoming impossible or "unthinkable," or that, if it broke out, it could not last

tional" forces the exhortations of the moralists, the lessons of the historians, the prescriptions of the economists, have battled in vain. Human nature has continued to clasp to its bosom its "Great Illusion" and to be governed by its "irrational prejudices." How, then, in face of this leading feature of the history of the modern world, can we rationally hope that a still greater freedom of intercourse and multiplicity of contacts should reverse the tendency to increasing strength of the national spirit? It remains true in general that, the more we know of other peoples, the more we prefer our own.

more than a few months; because of the economic chaos that must ensue, and the economic exhaustion of the nations at war. If men had continued to be governed in the same degree as in peace by strictly economic motives, these prophecies would have been justified. But the economists had failed to take into their calculations the all-important fact that, on the outbreak of war, the balance of motives sustaining the activities of men would be at once profoundly altered. In vast numbers of men, the economic motive, so dominant in peace, fell to a very subordinate position, and capitalists, professional men, artisans, and laborers alike, were dominated (with, of course, many exceptions) by patriotic and other war-sustaining motives. Viscount Milner writes: "the general conviction certainly was, and it was strongest on the part of men versed in economic studies, that, if nothing else brought the war to an early close, the impossibility of financing it must do so. In view of the enormous costliness of modern warfare, it was argued, and reasonably argued that no great civilized country could long endure the financial strain." And he cites other instances in which, as he says, "actual experience, in and after the war, has confounded even the best-reasoned economic anticipations." ("Questions of the Hour.")

LECTURE III

THE Anarchic and the Cosmopolitan ideals, then, are alike in that they both are compatible with a universal code and more especially with the Christian code; the formulation and advocacy of them have been mainly due to the promptings of Christian ethics.

Both these ideals, which demand for their realization the complete repudiation of national ethics, have, like the universal ethics out of which they spring, one very grave defect, not hitherto mentioned, which we must now consider at some length. Namely, they assume that all men and all races of men are for all practical purposes essentially alike; they accept literally as an axiomatic truth the dogma that "all men are created equal"; and they interpret the dogma, not only in the sense that all existing men have equal claims upon

73

their fellows for justice, for humane and considerate treatment, but also in the much more questionable sense that all men and all races of men are endowed in an equal degree with the same capacities and tendencies, that all alike have by nature the same potentialities. They assume that the immense differences we observe between men and races of men are due only to differences in the degrees to which these identical native potentialities are realized; these differences of degree of realization being in turn due to differences of circumstance and opportunity. The advocate of universal ethics, starting with this dogmatic assumption, and contemplating instances in which individuals have risen to lofty heights of moral and intellectual achievement, deduces from these premises the belief that all men are equally capable of attaining similar heights; and he is apt to believe and to assert that only the prevalence of the spirit of nationality prevents the universal elevation of mankind to these same moral and intellectual levels. On this belief he founds his indictment of national ethics and his demand that it be wholly swept away in favor of the universal system.

The objections that, up to this point, I have raised against the universal system would all be valid, even though this basic assumption of the system were true. That is to say, even if it were literally true that all men are created equal, are endowed with exactly similar potentialities of moral and intellectual development, those difficulties and weaknesses which I have already pointed out would remain inherent in any universal or cosmopolitan system. My argument has been one of deduction from the nature of man as a social being, from those features which are common to men of all times and all races. In answer, it might be urged that, in spite of those objections to any and every universal system, whether anarchic or cosmopolitan, some such system must be accepted as our ethical ideal, an ideal which should shape and govern all political endeavor. For, it may be argued, though the innate bases of human nature are relatively fixed and immutable, yet man is a rational being and is, during his long period of youth, very plastic, very susceptible to the moral influences about him, is, in fact, liable to be molded by them to a degree which renders the innate factors of his constitution well-nigh negligible. In support of this contention, the universalist may point, with Benjamin Kidd, to the remarkable success of the German State in molding, by the aid of the Hegelian philosophy, all its citizens to the moral (or amoral) pattern desired and designed by it. He may point also to the golden age of the Antonines, when all the many tribes and races within the Roman Empire dwelt peacefully and prosperously together.

Let us grant a considerable force to such arguments; let us admit that in the moral sphere man is very plastic, if only he be brought under the exclusive influence of a consistent and harmonious moral tradition; and that, therefore, if the universal system could once be established in undisputed sway, it might maintain itself for a considerable period.

We have now to inquire, whether, granting this moral plasticity of men to be great enough to render possible a universal system, such a system would be the truly desirable or best.

The phase of the argument upon which we now enter aims to show that, even if the universal system of ethics could be established and maintained throughout the world, in either its anarchic or its cosmopolitan form, and even if the system so established should be found to add greatly to the happiness and prosperity of the mass of mankind, it still would not be one of which we could approve. If, under such a regime, the precepts common to all the universal ethical systems were faithfully observed by all men; if we all obeyed strictly the precepts of the Sermon on the Mount; if we all treated every man, not at all as means, but only as an end in himself; if all of us always acted for the greatest good of the greatest number of our existing fellow-men; still I say we should not have achieved a morality which our reason could approve. Our morality would be fatally defective. In other words, I wish to show that any and every strictly and purely universal ethical system holds up a false ideal.

Here let me admit that this demonstration rests upon an assumption which is by no means accepted by all moral philosophers, namely, the validity in ethics of the Utilitarian principle broadly and rightly conceived. Many of the moralists, perhaps the majority of them, have rejected the Utilitarian principle as the foundation of ethics. They have maintained that the precepts of ethics can and must be deduced from some *a priori* principle, some moral axiom or axioms which, in virtue of some factor of our constitution, we are compelled to accept, or do naturally or supernaturally and inevitably accept. This alleged factor of our constitution has been very variously described, by some as "the moral sense," by others as "the conscience," by others as "Reason," and in various other ways too numerous to be mentioned here. In spite of these differences between the moral philosophers I speak of, they all have this one feature in common, namely, they repudiate the Utilitarian principle; that is to say they repudiate the view that ethical precepts must be judged and evaluated in terms of the consequences which result from the practice of them. Few of the opponents of the Utilitarian principle have made this repudiation explicitly; they have not singled out for criticism and rejection this essential feature of Utilitarianism; rather they have avoided this essential feature and have indulged in elaborate criticism of the errors which, unfortunately, have been so generally mixed in with the Utilitarian principle by its exponents. For most of the exponents of the Utilitarian philosophy have followed its founder,

Jeremy Bentham, in incorporating with it, in addition to its essential principle, two very serious errors.

Its essential principle is that ethical precepts must be judged in the light of the consequences which result from the practice of them. To this Bentham and his followers added, first, that the only consequences thus to be taken into account are the increase or diminution of the quantity of human happiness: secondly, they added the hedonist error, the assertion that the motive of all human action is the desire to secure pleasure or to avoid pain. The Utilitarians of the strict school usually committed themselves to yet a third serious error, namely, they identified happiness with pleasure or a succession of pleasures. I have no space here to expound the enormity of this error and the great difference between happiness and pleasure. I must refer the reader to my discussion of this topic in "Introduction to Social Psychology."

The critics of Utilitarianism, instead of examining its essential principle, have concentrated their attacks upon these two adventitious supplements, the second of which, as is now generally agreed, is simply a false though plausible assertion, while the former is a highly questionable presumption.

And, though so many moral philosophers have pretended to reject the Utilitarian principle, by far the greater number of these rejectors accept it implicitly and surreptitiously: for they discuss the nature of the Good or the highest Good, conceived as the goal of moral endeavor; and, in attempting to define the Good, they clearly are seeking to define that state of mankind which moral endeavor must strive to realize, they are seeking to define ethical conduct and ethical precepts in terms of their consequences for human life.

It is inconceivable that any sane man, however sophisticated, would approve ethical precepts of a kind which must tend to the general degradation of human nature and to the destruction of civilization and of all higher culture. But just that must be the tendency of universal ethics, if strictly applied and generally practised; as I now proceed to show.

We may best ascertain the natural tendencies of any ethical system by imagining it to have attained to complete dominance over all rivals and to have exerted its influence to the fullest extent possible throughout a considerable period, say a century.

Let us, then, imagine a universal system to have been established and to have worked in the most harmonious and successful way throughout the world. All national boundaries and distinctions have been, we suppose, abolished, and, with them, all the irrational preferences and prejudices of race and nationality. With the abolition of nationality, war and the danger of war have been removed, and the world is profoundly at peace. All countries of the world are open equally to all men; and the precepts of universal ethics are universally applied and observed, under an anarchic order or a world-wide cosmopolitan government.

Let me first depict what seem to me the inevitable consequences of this state of affairs; and then seek to justify the picture by adducing the evidence provided by history, biology, and psychology. And the picture may with advantage be drawn on two scales, a larger and a smaller, the world scale and the local scale of a particular territory.

Consider, then, the large-scale consequences of the general practice of universal ethics during one century. The outstanding consequence, beside and beneath which all others would appear insignificant and subordinate, would be an immense multiplication of the peoples of the lower cultures. By the end of the century (unless in the meantime the whole apparatus of applied science and administration had broken down, bringing in consequence widespread disasters destructive of human life on a vast scale) the population of the world would have become at least three times as numerous as at present, rising to the neighborhood of some 5000 millions.[1] And of these 5000 millions the great majority would be descended from the peoples now enjoying the more primitive forms of culture. The populations which have created, and which at the present time are the chief bearers of, scientific culture and administration would not have substantially increased; in all probability they would have actually diminished in number—if they still remained a distinguishable part of the whole. But they would not remain a distinguishable part.

[1] This is a very modest estimate. It has recently been calculated that, if the present average rate of increase of population should continue for two centuries, the population of the world would at the end of that time be multiplied tenfold, that is to say it would be about 16,000 millions.

This vast population would not be, as is the present population, very unevenly distributed over the surface of the world. Rather, freedom to emigrate or wander and the great facilities of transportation, characteristic of the modern age, would have distributed this population throughout the world, in a manner that would secure in each area a density of population proportioned to its natural resources and to its capacity for the support of human life. The great fertile spaces of the Americas, of Africa, and of Australia would be filled; in all areas where reserves of water-power or of other great natural sources of energy are most accessible, the population would be very dense; and, in all these areas, the population would be the product of multiple race-crossings. People of the most diverse origins would have mingled together on terms of perfect social equality, separated by no prejudices of race or nation, by no barriers of castes or social classes. This means that inter-marriage of the most diverse stocks would have taken place on a vast scale; so that, after the lapse of a century of such mingled existence, miscegenation would be far advanced or, perhaps, completed; and the remnant of the peoples that have built up our modern civilization would have been absorbed in the general mass, like a few drops of milk in a basin of coffee, leaving upon that mass hardly any recognizable trace of their racial qualities.

This forecast of the effects of a century of universal ethics, generally and literally obeyed, is based upon four assumptions; they may be stated as follows: (1) Under the conditions of universal freedom and of political and social equality postulated by the universal ethics, population would tend rapidly to distribute itself over the surface of the earth in the way suggested; (2) peoples of lower cultures would multiply rapidly; (3) while those of higher culture would not, but, rather, in all probability would dwindle rapidly in numbers; (4) miscegenation would result. It is now my task to show that these four assumptions are well-founded.

1. We have only recently entered upon the era of extreme facility of human transportation on a large scale; yet already we have good evidence of its effects in promoting vast migrations. Wherever no bars to migration into the less crowded areas have been raised, the people of the crowded areas have begun to swarm in; and

especially into such areas as are under administrations that effectively protect the weak against the strong. Already these modern facilities of transport have produced migrations far exceeding, in respect of numbers, anything recorded in the previous history of mankind. Consequently, in all such areas, in defiance of Universal Ethics, certain restrictions have already been imposed; in some, as Australia, absolute restrictions; in others, as in North America and South Africa, partial restrictions.

Against these barriers the crowded peoples are already protesting loudly, clamoring for their removal. Chinese and Japanese have shown the strongest tendency of this kind; but the 300 millions of India are not indifferent. They have shown their mobility and have begun to swarm into Africa; and they have been prevented from swarming into America and Australia only by severe and rigid exclusion laws. It seems safe to suppose that, if no such barriers had been raised, North America and Australia and South and East Africa would already have been made the homes of many millions of Asiatics, both yellow and brown.

2. There can be no doubt that, where climatic

conditions permitted (and that would be over most of the great areas mentioned) these immigrants, settling in millions in these favored and relatively uncrowded regions, and augmented in numbers by a steady full stream of further immigration, would breed at a great rate. They would in the main retain the low standard of living and the high standard of laboriousness to which they have been inured through many centuries; for their numbers would preclude all possibility of any rapid transformation of their standards. And, living under western administration, they would, so long as this was maintained, be protected more or less completely from the great checks by which, in all former ages and in all parts of the world, increase of population has been severely restrained, namely, war, pestilence, famine, abortion, and infanticide. For western administration, applied according to the principles of universal ethics, would abolish war and famine, would reduce the death-rate from disease to a minimum, would strictly prevent infanticide and abortion (the two greatest and most general causes of the restriction of population among peoples of the lower culture) [1] and would

[1] Cf. A. M. Carr-Saunders, "The Population Problem," Oxford, 1922.

make early marriage and the raising of large families relatively easy to all men.

India shows us clearly that the prime and chief effect of bringing such populations under western administration is to multiply them at a great rate. Such administration has been only partially and locally established in India, with increasing efficiency, throughout a period of hardly one century; yet already the effect has been to increase the population from 100 millions to more than 300 millions. Japan, during the brief period since the introduction of administration of the western type, has shown a similar tendency to very rapid increase of numbers. Java, under the excellent administration of the Dutch, illustrates the same fact; for Java, with nearly 35 millions, is now, after a century of such administration, one of the most densely populated regions of the earth. [1]

[1] It is now made a ground of complaint in India and Japan, a complaint that threatens to grow louder and more urgent, that their populations are not allowed to emigrate freely to Africa, America, and other of the less crowded regions of the earth. Those who raise these complaints commonly claim that such emigration is needed to relieve the pressure of the remaining population upon the means of subsistence. But, so long as these peoples continue to breed at the "natural" rate, the largest conceivable emigration would not appreciably relieve the pressure in the home-countries or improve the lot of their inhabitants. I cite in this connection the following

3. The populations that have created and established among themselves western administration and the arts of modern civilization would find themselves in economic competition with this rapidly increasing horde of population of very much lower standards of living. And experience shows clearly how in the main such people would react to the situation. There would be, for the vast majority of them, a choice between two

---

passage from Mr. William Archer's eminently wise and sympathetic study of Indian conditions ("India and the Future," 1917): "There are, between Kashmir and Cape Comorin, over three hundred million people. Suppose 4 per cent of them, or 12,000,000, were to emigrate, what difference would that make to India? In a single decade (supposing no very grave calamity to intervene) the population would have risen at least to its former level. But 12,000,000 is very little short of the whole white population of South Africa, Australia, and Canada. Is it for a moment to be imagined that these countries would submit to having their whole policy, their conditions of life and course of development, altered by such a huge influx of an alien and unassimilable race? Of course, this is a flagrantly impossible contingency; but that only makes it all the clearer that no emigration which is practically conceivable would sensibly ameliorate Indian conditions. Any outflow that should be at all perceptible in India would mean, in other countries, an inflow amounting to a cataclysm. But suppose emigration on a large scale were possible—suppose, say, that a new India could be set apart in Africa, capable of absorbing a million immigrants a year for the next half century—would that be a real and permanent benefit to the Motherland? On the contrary it would be a misfortune. It would indefinitely adjourn the day when India shall realize that life is to be valued by its quality, not by its quantity, and that a country which would be master of its fate must first be master of its instincts. Of course, this is a lesson that many other peoples are far from having taken to heart; but India has not

alternatives only: (a) to lower greatly their standard of living; (b) to restrict their breeding very severely, to deny themselves the luxury of children save in very severely restricted numbers. That the latter would be the choice most commonly made we cannot doubt. It is consistent with all we know of human nature;

---

even begun to learn it. She is still unquestioningly devoted to that religion of fecundity which she must one day modify unless she is prepared to conquer the world.

"Let it be clearly realized that this is no mere rhetorical phrase. The world, indeed is not yet overfilled; but the limits of possible expansion are being rapidly approached; and practically all desirable territory is staked-out by people who naturally propose to reserve it for development along the lines of their own racial tradition. It is quite certain that only by force of arms can this right of reservation be infringed; and its successful infringement, in a series of 'folk-wanderings,' would mean a relapse into chaos. . . .   Sooner or later, at all events, the pinch must come, and India must learn that her salvation lies, not in numerical expansion, whether within or without her boundaries, but in the intensification and ennoblement of life." And Mr. Archer goes on to show how distinguished writers on Indian problems, as on so many other human problems, are led to make foolish and solemn statements by their neglect to grasp or consider the fundamental facts of population and the processes of procreation. Nine-tenths of the literature of politics and of social reform seem to be written by persons ignorant of the fact that every human being is born of a woman and begotten by a man. There is now no excuse for this ignorance. Let every social reformer begin his studies by reading Mr. Harold Cox's "The Problem of Population." This is no abstruse study, but a plain statement of the A, B, C of the matter. The impossibility of improving the lot of the peoples of India by emigration, is redoubled or trebled, when we reflect that China and Japan are similarly overcrowded areas.

and in America we have had an impressive demonstration of this effect.[1] An educated intelligent population that has attained to a high standard of living will not consent to the

[1] F. A. Walker ("Discussions in Economics and Statistics," New York, 1899) has shown that the tides of more recent immigration have produced this effect upon the older American stock in a very pronounced degree. The validity of General Walker's demonstration has been questioned. But, in a recent discussion of the question, Prof. H. P. Fairchild ("Immigration," p. 225) shows that a number of experts have confirmed it. He shows in fact that, although it may be impossible to make the reasoning which points to this conclusion convincing to the prejudiced and unintelligent reader, the conclusion is supported by a consensus of expert opinion. Prof. Fairchild goes so far as to maintain, in the light of all the available evidence, that "if immigration has not positively lessened our population, we may be certain that it has failed to increase it to any considerable extent. Its net result, so far as size of population is concerned, has been to substitute a very large foreign element from various sources, for a native element which would otherwise have come into being." If this has been true of the immigration of the 19th century, or the "older immigration," it seems only too probable that it will prove true in still higher degree of the "new immigration." That is to say that, unless some radical changes of law and custom should greatly alter the present trend of affairs, the population of the United States will, at the end of the present century, be one in which the blood of the old American stock (of predominantly Nordic race) will be hardly at all represented; it will be a population formed by the blending of descendants of Southeastern Europeans, and of Turks, Armenians, Negroes, Mexicans, etc.

It is not unreasonable to suppose that the presence of the Negro population of the Southern States has had a similar effect, namely, has restricted the multiplication of the white stock and that, if Negroes had never been brought into North America, the country would have produced, in place of its ten or more millions of Negroes, an approximately equal number of white people in addition to those now existing.

reduction of that standard; and it will not bring children into the world to live according to a reduced standard. [1]

If the immigration of some few millions of Europeans of slightly lower standards of living has had a profound effect of this kind in America, even before the end of the nineteenth century,

---

[1] Of European countries, France, whose people have for so many centuries led the vanguard of civilization, is already the scene of a strongly working tendency to substitution of population.

Mr. Sisley Huddleston, in a recent article (Christian Science Monitor, August 4, 1923) writes of "the dwindling native population [of France], with the corresponding encouragement to immigration" as "one of the gravest problems which presents itself to France." "It is estimated," he says, "that 150,000 Polish workers are with their families in France. The other Slav countries have not yet sent many workers to France, but the inflow is beginning and it is easy to foresee that in a few years there will be at least 1,000,000 Slavs. . . . There are Greeks and Turks, Hungarians and men of the Levant; there are scattered all over the country contingents of Italians." He says nothing of the contingents of colored "Frenchmen"; but he writes: "While the native population remains unequal to the proper exploitation of the potential resources of France, it will be obligatory to recruit labor power from beyond the French frontiers." Even from his narrow economic standpoint (which leads him to use the word "obligatory" in the absurd way in which other economists speak of "economic laws" as something beyond the control of human will) he discerns a danger in this process. "The danger from the point of view of the French artisan is that these immigrants are generally subdued and amenable, and must tend, therefore, to reduce the whole standard of living which has been hardly won by the French trade-unions." But he does not seem to be aware of the greater danger, namely, that the process is a vicious circle, that not only does the low birth-rate encourage immigration, but that also the swelling tide of immigration discourages the native birth-rate.

can we doubt that, when confronted with a much larger number of immigrants with a much lower standard of living and a 'natural' rate of increase, the American people (and others similarly situated) would exhibit the same phenomenon in a highly intensified degree? [1]

[1] Mr. C. R. Noyes, discussing this topic in a recent article ("The Weather Chart of Population," Yale Review, July, 1923) writes: "The United States lie between these two areas of high pressure [Europe and Eastern Asia]. Here are found the greatest developed resources and the greatest industries in the world. Therefore this land is able, both through its agriculture and its industry, to support a larger population than any similar area. Yet we have but 35 people to the square mile. To be sure, it is this extraordinarily low ratio of people to means of subsistence which makes possible our comparatively high standard of living. On the other hand, this very standard is the attraction that makes our country the natural objective of all superfluous population. If we should resume our old policy of granting asylum to the oppressed of the earth, if we should again welcome immigrants to our shores as we have done in the past, it is certain that they would offer themselves at a rate hitherto unexampled. For never before in our history has there existed on other shores of both the Atlantic and the Pacific the dynamic pressure of population that is now beginning to make itself felt in Asia as well as in Europe. . . . In the United States it is not too late to forestall the process of overcrowding and to fix ourselves for centuries at that stage in which the whole people, retaining their soundness and sanity through the necessity for work, have, because of the sparseness of the population, the abundance of resources, the advanced state of the arts and the initial advantage of a relative equality of opportunity, a chance to combine the virtues of the aristocratic with those of the pioneer society. But population seeks its level, and only by building dykes on the Dutch pattern can we reclaim our lands from an inundation which would gradually obliterate the splendid foundations that have been laid for a social structure designed for 'the greatest good of the greatest number.'

4. That miscegenation of the completest kind would result from these conditions, if they could be realized, it is impossible to doubt. Wherever different races have lived in the same area, cross-breeding has occurred to a considerable extent; it has occurred even where race-prejudice has been strong and where severe social and legal bars have been placed upon intermarriage of the races. How then should it not take place very freely where many different races would be closely intermingled, where all social and legal bars to intermarriage would be removed, and where the prevalent ethical sentiment would

---

The barbarian invasion of ancient times has given place to the peaceful penetration of the low-class immigrant from an overcrowded land. But the cause and the effect are the same, though the manner is different. And the danger is that to-day this flow can take place almost unnoticed. No force is required. No vandal armies precede the host. There is no apparent threat in these docile steerage passengers. For the same improvements in transportation which have consolidated the societies of the world into one, have removed the friction in the way of movements of masses of men. The barriers are down and the channels are wide. . . . From these various considerations bearing upon the social and economic interests of the American people, and in furtherance of a full realization of the possibilities of an exceptional natural opportunity, it seems high time to establish the principle of the exclusion of further immigration as a national doctrine. The 'melting pot' already holds all it can well digest for some time to come; and in the face of the threatening influx, the present temporary and half-way measures should be replaced by uncompromising and permanent restriction."

favor, rather than discourage, such inter-marriage?[1]

A century (or at most two centuries) of the sway of universal ethics, untempered by any remnant of national ethics, would result in the practical extinction of the white race in all of the two Americas, and in Africa, Australia, and Asia; the dwindling remnant being absorbed wholly in the flood of colored peoples.

It is probable that in Europe descendants of the present populations would survive for a longer period; but there also they would be but a dwindling remnant. The absence of unoccu-pied lands and the existing density of population would retard the influx of other races. But, even without any such influx, the peoples of Europe would feel severely the economic com-petition of untold millions of lower culture and

[1] The extent to which cross-breeding has taken place and still is going on between the Negro and the white races in the United States cannot be stated with any precision; estimates differ widely. It seems to be widely assumed in the North that the process came to an end with slavery. On the other hand, a number of colored correspondents have assured me that it is still going on rapidly; and they, perhaps, are in a better position for the formation of opinion on this question than most white men can be. It seems obvious that the recent rapid migration of colored people into the northern states, which seems likely to continue, must tend to ac-celerate greatly the process of cross-breeding.

lower standards of living, organized in vast industrial armies in all other parts of the world.[1] And the indirect competition of these masses would in all probability have, on their reproduction rate, the same effect as that exerted in other areas by the more direct competition of immigrants. England and Germany, for example, already populated far beyond the point at which they can maintain their standard of living without vast exportation of manufactured goods, would find, as they are already finding, the world increasingly closed to their exports; just because the rest of the world would produce what it needed at a lower cost, by reason of vast reserves of labor accustomed to low standards of living.

Lancashire is already feeling the competition of the cotton mills of India, China, and Japan, and is likely, under any regime, to find this competition increasingly severe. And, under the sway of the universal system, the process would be vastly accelerated; until the Lancashire weavers, and also the workers in many other industries

[1] In the way foretold by the late Charles Pearson in his "National Life and Character," (1893) a book which in its day was very widely read. Pearson seems to have over-estimated the rate of the changes which he foretold, neglecting to give due weight to the counteracting influence of the spirit of nationalism.

who live largely by the export of their products, would not only lose their foreign markets but also find their home markets invaded by the products of labor of lower standards. And, under the system whose results we are forecasting, protective tariffs would be out of the question.

But, in the absence of all restrictions, the European area would not remain without its immigrants. In European countries there are many forms of labor that can be effectively undertaken by coolies from China, Japan, India, and Africa. Hitherto the prevalence of race-prejudice has served as a more or less effective check on such immigration. If this check were removed entirely, we should soon have a variegated population throughout Europe. Chinese laundrymen, Japanese gardeners and domestics, Negro laborers, Indian road-sweepers, would be found everywhere. After no long time, the old European, like the present-day American, would scorn to undertake unskilled labor. He would increasingly confine himself to the white-collar occupations; his numbers would then dwindle, making room for still more immigrants. France is already giving an ill-considered encouragement to such immigration of Negroes from her vast African dominions; and, having largely overcome her race-prejudices, she seems likely to lead the European peoples along the primrose path of domestic comfort, miscegenation and race-suicide.

The forecast which I have sketched of the inevitable results of the prevalence of the universal ethics is, I think, well founded. It is not possible to forecast the results in detail or to foretell with accuracy the rate at which the forecasted changes would proceed. But that the tendency to such changes would be strong and would realize itself sooner or later, seems to me an indisputable proposition.

What attitude, then, can the exponent of unmitigated universal ethics assume towards this tendency, which the general acceptance of his principles must bring into operation? If he is honest and consistent, and if he resolutely rejects the Utilitarian principle, he can only say— "My principles are right, and, being eternal principles, they must be followed regardless of consequences. What we have to do is to face and accept these consequences bravely, endeavoring to raise all mankind in the scale of civilization. We must strain every nerve to educate, to civilize, to spread our culture among all the peoples of the world, so that, when our stock disappears from the scene, all that is worthy of preservation, all that it has contributed of permanent value, our science, our art, our literature, our industrial skill, and our free political institutions, shall be preserved and, in the world-civilization which is to succeed us, shall be incorporated in the cosmopolitan State which is to supersede our petty nationalisms." Like Mr. H. G. Wells, he may sketch fanciful pictures (attractive perhaps to some minds) of a completely civilized, industrialized, and cosmopolitan world, a world in which swarms of variegated and parti-colored men and women pullulate in vast cities of steel and glass, cities provided with the most wonderful systems of free transportation, free education, free recreation, and free love. That is to say, he may indulge the dream that the civilized fraction of mankind is capable of leavening with its culture the whole of the human race, of assimilating it, even while that civilized fraction itself declines to the point of extinction; so that, as it dwindles away, it may see its ethical and its political culture, its art and science and literature, carried onward and upward by the populations whom it has taught to appreciate their value.

This would be an idle dream indeed. It is not necessary for me to spend any time in arguing against the possibility of its realization. The experience of America, in its efforts to assimilate, to Americanize, a few millions from the south and east of Europe has been sufficiently illuminating. And there is more than sufficient reason to believe that, the more the immigrants are unlike the native stock in race and culture, the more difficult is the task of assimilation. If America had assimilated the bulk of the Negroes who have dwelt within her borders for more than a century, making only one-tenth of her population, the hope of assimilating the whole world would still be fantastically vain.

When our optimistic exponents of universal ethics describe in glowing terms the future of our civilization, they presumably base their expectations, so far as they can be said to think at all, on an amiable view of the relations between Europeans and the peoples of lower cultures which seems to have been widely entertained about the middle of the nineteenth century. Public attention had been drawn to certain striking instances, notably the Red Men of North America and the natives of Australia and Tasmania and of other islands of the Pacific, in which the aboriginal populations seemed to fade mysteriously away at contact with the white man. It was complacently assumed that this was the natural and inevitable fate of all the colored peoples; and that the duty of the white race towards them should consist merely in comforting the declining remnants of all such races, making their disappearance from the earth as little distressing as possible, and converting them first by missionary effort, so that, as they passed away, they might at least enjoy the consolations of Christianity.[1] But we know now that this was an ill-based anticipation. We know something of the causes of such disappearance of some of the peoples of lower culture; and we know that many such peoples do not thus fade away. In fact it seems probable that, if all of them had been treated from the first on the principles of universal ethics, all of these races would still be with us, and would have

[1] This complacent view, so characteristic of the Victorian age, is reflected e.g. in the writings of the late Benjamin Kidd.

steadily increased in numbers under the fostering care of a paternal administration.

We cannot too clearly realize that one of the greatest achievements of our scientific civilization is the lowering of the death-rate by the conquest of various diseases, by the maintenance of an efficient public health-service, by the spread of a knowledge of the elementary principles of hygiene, and by the prevention of famines due to local scarcity by use of modern means of transportation. These great agencies for the lowering of the death-rate have only recently come into world-wide operation. But their very partial application during the last century, in such an area as British India, has sufficed to treble the population of that area.

The maintenance of such services in an increasingly efficient manner has become a chief part of the white man's burden: and the chief result of the bearing of that burden has been that the burden has become three times as heavy. Under the universal system of ethics, the efforts and resources of the whole world would inevitably and increasingly be absorbed in this gigantic task. By an immense and sustained effort, the cosmopolitan State might bring down the death-rate everywhere to the low level now obtaining in England or New England. The more successful the World-State might prove in maintaining in all regions an efficient administration of the western or scientific kind, the lower would be the death-rate, and the more the birth-rate would rise among the populations of the lower standards of living. A moderate degree of such success would ensure for them a rate of increase that would far surpass every rate hitherto realized. We might hope to achieve a universal death-rate of 10 per 1000; and this might well go with a birth-rate of 50 per 1000 (or more) among the populations of low standards of life. These populations would then double their numbers every twenty years or so; and, so long as the burden was successfully carried, its weight would increase at this staggering rate.

The Universalist will admit that this would be an impossible state of affairs. But he will argue that, as the peoples of lower culture are brought more completely under the beneficent influences of western administration, they will learn two things and, in so doing, profoundly modify the situation. First, he may say, they

will learn to restrict their birth-rate; as the
peoples of Europe and North America have been
learning to do during the last fifty years.
Secondly, they will learn to carry their burden
for themselves; that is to say they will be
assimilated to the point at which they can
effectively maintain for themselves the public
services and the private standards of life which
are the very framework and basis of modern
civilization.

It may be admitted that these anticipations
might be partially realized; but only very partially. The probabilities require to be stated
in terms of two different assumptions; (a) the
common Universalist assumption that all men
are created equal; (b) the assumption that men
and the various races of men are unequally
endowed with the qualities that render possible
the attainment of a high standard of life.

Accepting for the moment the former assumption, let us consider the consequences. The
population of the world would increase very
rapidly; and each part of it would increase the
more rapidly, the lower the standard of life it had
attained. The population of the whole world
would eventually adjust its birth-rate to the

means of subsistence, and then would settle down to develop the higher culture.   And, though this population would in the main be derived from the peoples which at present are lowest in the scale of culture, that result may be contemplated with equanimity; since (by the hypothesis) all men are equal and one man is as good as another. Only an irrational race-prejudice could lead us to regret that the physical features of this population would be very different from those of the European type. If their souls glowed with the light of intellect and the warmth of a lofty morality, what more could be desired?   The dying out of the stocks which at present are the bearers of our civilization would merely mean that the establishment of a settled world-order of uniformly high civilization would be postponed for a few generations or, perhaps, for a few centuries.

But, even on the assumption that all men are created equal, this view would be unduly optimistic.   As I pointed out in a previous lecture, human nature develops its higher potentialities only when men live as members of stable communities, cemented by strong moral and political traditions.   The process that in this country is called "assimilation" is the process of imparting such traditions to the immigrants. Does not American experience clearly prove that, even when the material to be assimilated is not very unlike the assimilators and in numbers does not exceed a small percentage of them, the process is slow and difficult. [1]

Under the conditions we have imagined, the assimilation process would be very much more difficult than any that America has hitherto undertaken. For, all barriers to migration having been removed, North America would very soon contain many millions of immigrants of all colors and creeds, of the most diverse traditions, and of relatively low standards; and the same would be true of all the areas which at present are relatively uncrowded. And the difficulty of assimilation would have been very greatly increased; for the strongest of all aids to assimilation would have been destroyed in the process of denationalization required by the Universal Ethics. That strongest agency of assimilation is the spirit of nationality, the pride in America's institutions and in her past history,

[1] Cp. A. Drachsler "Assimilation and Immigration" and many similar studies.

and the hope for her future as a mighty and beneficent power among the nations of the world, in short,
pride and hope in all those fine things symbolized
by the Stars and Stripes. All these emotions and
sentiments, which are of the essence of nationality,
are repugnant to the Universal Ethics and would
have been destroyed at its bidding. The immigrant could no longer be moved by the desire to
become a true American, by pride in his citizenship in the greatest nation in the world, by
aspiration to maintain and promote the greatness
of his adopted country. He would be a citizen
not of any one country, but of the Cosmopolitan State; national pride, national aspiration,
and national service would be merely memories
of the dark and dreadful past, memories of that
period in which we now live, perplexed and
tormented by the conflict between the demands
of our Universal Ethics and the claims of the
Nation upon our loyalty to its traditions and
its ideals.

SUPPLEMENTARY NOTE TO LECTURE III

The extent of ignorance and blindness and the
extreme diversity of opinions in respect of the
most fundamental of all political and social

problems, namely the problems of population, are astonishing. They are due, no doubt, to the fact that any contact with these problems is apt to bring into play emotional tendencies that strongly distort or repress all intellectual activity in relation to them.

This influence is amusingly illustrated by the opinions expressed by contemporary writers on the work of Malthus. While many eminent authors contemptuously refer to his famous treatise on population as a tissue of exploded fallacies, others express the highest praise, regarding it as the beginning of all wisdom in Sociology. I have more sympathy with the latter than with the former. The truth seems to be that, while the forecasts made or implied by Malthus have, up to the present time, been largely falsified by the incidence of new factors not foreseen by him, especially the exploitation of the earth's natural reserves of energy, nevertheless, his fundamental assumptions hold good, and that, unless the physicists and synthetic chemists shall shortly put at our disposal vast new sources of energy and food, every civilized administration must become increasingly concerned with the principles taught by Malthus.

Another striking illustration of the extent and perversity of contemporary blindness to the rudimentary facts of human reproduction is the almost complete absence of any intelligent reference to them in the floods of printed matter concerning the relations of France with Germany. Many influential German writers have boldly affirmed that, since the German population continues to increase rapidly, Germany is entitled to overrun the territories of other peoples. This in short was the keynote of the justification offered for her outrageous outbreak of 1914 and of her demand for a place in the sun. And they have loudly asserted that the absence of any similar increase of the population of France marks her as a decadent nation and the natural prey of her eastern neighbor. The war has sufficiently refuted this last proposition. For it has shown the French to be the most vigorous and virile of all existing peoples. And this is what might properly have been expected in the light of any unprejudiced consideration of the facts. For, while the other leading nations have, for some generations, been breeding chiefly from the lowest strata, the French, having adopted the small-family-system throughout all the social strata, have avoided this source of national degeneration and have maintained the quality of their population. Hence the astonishing energy, resolution, and resistant power of the French in the Great War. During the war, I had opportunities to observe in France large numbers of British and French troops and of German prisoners, and I was much impressed by the appearance of a more uniformly good standard of physique and mentality among the French soldiers, the relative absence among them of the poor specimens so common among the British and the Germans.

In spite of the lessons of the War, publicists of all degrees of eminence still seem inclined to follow the late Marquis of Salisbury in regarding the French as decadent, because they are too intelligent to produce a swarm of population for which they cannot provide without overrunning the territories of other peoples. There is also manifest a tendency to accept the claims still made in Germany on the ground of her continued increase of population. Germany, while professing inability to pay her just debts and complaining of the economic hardships suffered by her population, continues to indulge herself in the greatest and most expensive luxury that any people can enjoy, namely a high birth-rate. It is, I think, substantially true to say that Germany deliberately brought on the Great War by discouraging emigration and encouraging the increase of her home-population. Yet in the main the difference between the rates of increase of population in France and in Germany, during the later part of the nineteenth century, was due to the fact that nature had given Germany immense and rich coal fields and had denied them to France. Germany converted her coal into the twenty millions or more of citizens by which the population of Germany exceeds that of France. What Mr. William Archer says of India is true also of Germany: "She is still unquestioningly devoted to that religion of fecundity which she must one day modify unless she is prepared to conquer the world." When the Germans complain of their inability to pay their debts, they are in the position of the pauper debtor who points to his large and still increasing family as his excuse for his default. To all such complaints France may justly reply in the wise words addressed to India by Mr. Archer: "A country which would be master of its fate must first be master of its instincts." And, when Germany demands to be excused from the payment of her debts, France may well reply in the words with which the same author comments upon the proposal that India should seek in emigration relief for the congestion of her population: "It would merely postpone the facing of her population problem, which she must assuredly undertake before she can claim her due place among the civilized nations of the world."

LECTURE IV

FURTHER DEMONSTRATION OF THE INSUFFICIENCY OF UNIVERSAL ETHICS

I HAVE tried to show you that, even on the most favorable assumption of human equality (the assumption that all men are potentially as good as the best, that every Hottentot, every dweller in the slums of Canton, of Madras, or of London, is by nature the equal of Washington and of Lincoln) the adoption of the universal system must quickly result in world-wide chaos; that, under any such system, civilization would everywhere give place to barbarism; that the whole world would fall into a condition comparable to that of Europe during the dark ages which followed the decay of the Roman Empire.

But the assumption that all men and all races are created equal is, as everyone knows, a false assumption. The inequalities of natural endowment among men of the same race are too great to be denied by any sane and impartial person; although some journalists of the ultra-democratic and cosmopolitan tendency love to repeat Jefferson's glittering generality and to ridicule those who do not share their prejudices, denouncing as anti-democratic snobbery all recognition of the fact of inequality. The recent application on a large scale of methods of mental measurement has merely made a little more definite our knowledge of the extent and distribution of these natural differences of mental endowment[1] among ourselves.

When we raise the same question in respect of the various branches of the human race, we are on more difficult ground. And we are on ground where the suggestion of differences of intrinsic value, or of level of natural endowment, arouses an even more violent opposition. It must be conceded that, so far as our knowledge goes, any existing people may be capable of producing individuals of the highest capacities of all kinds. But an impartial survey enables us to lay down with confidence the following propositions.

[1] Cp. especially "A Study of American Intelligence," by Carl Brigham, Princeton, 1922; and my "Is America Safe for Democracy?" N. Y., 1921.

1. Some races or peoples have been far more prolific than others in individuals that have displayed great capacities.

2. Some peoples have contributed far more than others to the development of culture; and some have proved their capacity to sustain for a time a high level of civilization, while the capacity of other peoples to do so remains unproved.

3. Among all peoples is a considerable proportion of individuals who do not easily assimilate the higher culture and who, therefore, do not and cannot contribute to the maintenance and further development of civilization, but rather require constant supervision and regulation, in order that they may be kept up to the standards of living required by civilization. And in some races or peoples the proportion of such individuals is very much higher than in others.

Now experience shows that, when any people attains to, or is brought under, western administration and enters upon the strenuous tasks of civilization, all parts of the population share in considerable degree, if not equally, those benefits which result in the lowering of the death-rate; and that, on the other hand, a differential birth-rate is apt very soon to appear. The less assimilable part of the population maintains a natural birth-rate; while the part which most effectively assimilates the current culture, which achieves the higher standard of living, and which plays the chief part in the services essential to the maintenance of civilization, this part shows a restricted birth-rate, a birth-rate so restricted that, in spite of a low death-rate, it hardly keeps up its numbers from generation to generation.

This phenomenon of the differential birth-rate, making for the relative increase of the unassimilable, is already manifested among all the peoples of European civilization and gives just ground for grave concern as to their future. But, if the universal system could be established throughout the world, the phenomenon would be manifested with very much greater intensity than it is by any existing people at the present time; and it would become world-wide. For everywhere the people of higher standards would be confronted by the economic competition of great masses of the relatively unassimilable. And, at the same time, there would be removed the principal in-

fluences which hitherto have in some degree counteracted this tendency, namely national pride,
pride of race, and pride of family.

It seems certain, then, that the undisputed
prevalence of the universal ethics would result in a rapid relative increase of the unassimilable of all races and peoples in all parts of the
world; and that the burden of administration
would rapidly become too great to be borne.
Intellectual and moral and material standards
would decline, and civilization would soon give
place to chaos.

There is yet another consideration which
must be taken into the account, although we
have no certain knowledge to go upon. I mean
the effects of miscegenation upon the qualities
of mankind. We have seen that, under the universal system, widespread miscegenation would
inevitably occur. We cannot confidently assert
that this would be injurious to the qualities of
the human race. Yet what knowledge we have
makes this seem highly probable. In the absence of knowledge, we have to be guided by
opinion. Almost all impartial observers are
agreed that the crossing of two human stocks
that are closely related may be expected to

produce a stock not inferior in any way to the parent stocks, and indeed one likely to be superior to them in the two important qualities of vigor and variability. But there is no less agreement in the more decided opinion that the crossing of widely unlike stocks is apt to produce a stock gravely inferior, even if the two parent stocks are of equal value. [1]

I lay no great stress on this consideration, since it remains possible (though improbable) that this ancient and widely held opinion is mistaken. [2]

The world-wide application of the principles of universal ethics would then greatly intensify a process which is already in operation in all civilized nations and which already gives occasion for the most serious concern; namely, the process of a dysgenically differential or adversely selective reproduction-rate. This process arrests

[1] In "Race or Mongrel," G. A. P. Schultz (Boston, 1908) brings together much evidence and reasoning of a somewhat loose nature in support of this ancient and widely held opinion. It has been confidently asserted by Herbert Spencer and expressed by such great democrats as President Eliot and Lord Bryce. Cp. also Reibmayr's "Inzucht und Vermischung beim Menschen."

[2] It is impossible to make exact allowance for the social handicap commonly suffered by Mulattoes, Eurasians, and all such progeny of widely diverse stocks, the handicap resulting from their lack of full participation in one firm social tradition.

the operation of natural selection, which, no matter how cruel it may have been in its effects upon individuals, has in the long run made for the improvement of the human race, for the increase of its intellectual capacities, and for the strengthening of the native tendencies that conduce to harmonious social life; and which also has weakened the tendencies that are incompatible with social welfare. And such a differential reproduction-rate not only arrests this conserving and improving tendency of natural selection, but also it puts in its place a tendency of the reverse kind, a tendency that makes for the lowering of the average intellectual and moral endowment of the population of each civilized country; in this way it renders each of such populations less capable in each succeeding generation of producing men of exceptionally high moral and intellectual endowments, those individuals whose activities are the only source of all further progress in the intellectual and the moral spheres, and without whom the level of civilization that we have already achieved cannot be maintained.

I will indicate this process of dysgenic selective reproduction within the nation only very briefly; because I have dwelt upon it at some length elsewhere,[1] and because many other writers have expounded its dangers, showing how it constitutes a most serious threat to the future of any nation in which it obtains and persists.

The tendency to dysgenic reproduction seems to come into operation in some degree as an inevitable consequence of the attainment by any nation of a certain level of civilization. It seems to have been a main factor in the destruction of most of the great nations and great civilizations of the past. It constitutes for the nations of the modern world a peculiarly serious threat, just because among them the principles of Universal Ethics are obtaining a greater influence than they have ever had in earlier ages.

There are two main factors which bring about this dysgenic selective reproduction. The one we may call psychological. It operates in some degree in all ages and in all civilizations. The other is ethical; it is a consequence of the sway of Universal Ethics, and is becoming increasingly powerful in the modern world.

---

[1] "Is America Safe for Democracy?" and "The Island of Eugenia, the Fantasy of a foolish Philosopher." Scribner's Magazine October, 1921.

The psychological factor is the exercise of intelligence in the regulation of marriage and reproduction. So long as men live on the plane of unreflecting obedience to custom, or, rather, so long as the instinctive promptings of men are regulated only or mainly by custom, and so long as the means of subsistence are ample, early marriage and unlimited procreation are the general customary rule of life.[1] But, as soon as culture develops and some part of the population begins to have leisure to reflect, this part begins to emancipate itself from the sway of instinct and of custom; and, unless the custom of early marriage and unlimited procreation is supported by the strong sanctions of a national religion and national ethics, one of the first effects of this emancipation is the exertion of intelligent control over the reproductive functions.

This intelligent control almost always aims at, and results in, a reduction of the labors and responsibilities of parenthood. Some men remain celibates, others marry late; and those

---

[1] The last condition has seldom been realized. We have seen an approximation to it in the United States of America in the colonial and early republican period.

who marry are apt to restrict the size of the family, more or less severely. And this tendency sets in earliest and works most strongly in those who have attained to some degree of leisure and culture; that is to say among those that constitute the upper social strata. On the other hand, those who remain subject to the sway of instinct and custom continue to propagate themselves at a more natural rate, that is to say a more rapid rate. Hence, in each generation, the bulk of the increase of population comes from the lower strata. And, all the while, in any society not regulated by strict rules of caste, individuals of exceptional capacity keep rising in the social scale to establish themselves in the upper strata; whereupon they and their descendants begin to exercise the intelligent control of reproduction that is the rule in these strata.

The ethical factor, the influence of a system of Universal Ethics, greatly accentuates this tendency. A well organized society swayed by such ethics is concerned for the welfare of all its members. It takes measures to prevent the natural consequences of unrestricted reproduction in its lower strata. It institutes vast schemes of poor-relief, of charity, of education, of free medical and surgical treatment in free hospitals, and of care for the health of all members of the community; bringing all the resources of modern science to its aid, it lowers the death-rate throughout the population, and, especially, it lowers the rate of infant mortality. In thus abolishing the high rate of infant mortality in the lower strata of society, it abolishes the one factor which, in earlier stages of social evolution, had counteracted in considerable degree the inequality of the birth-rates of the upper and lower strata, and so preserved in some measure the balance of numbers as between the upper and lower strata.[1]

Further, the influence of Universal Ethics works strongly to accentuate the dysgenic selective reproduction in two other ways.

The public services, which reduce the death-rate and facilitate for the lower strata the bearing and bringing up of large families, are

[1] I know, of course, that, in consequence of my plain statement of this fact, I shall be accused of advocating a high rate of infant mortality. I would ask that those of my readers who may feel moved to write to me, or to the press, denouncing me on this account, should first make an effort to reflect a little more logically on what I have written.

very costly; they can be maintained only by very large expenditure, which in turn means heavy taxation; and, in accordance with the principle that taxation shall fall upon those best able to bear it (a principle of Universal Ethics), it falls mainly upon those classes which have raised themselves in the social scale. The lowest strata then bring up large families; and the upper strata in the main bear the expense and, in consequence, restrict their own families the more severely.

The third way in which Universal Ethics contributes to accentuate the dysgenic selective reproduction has only in recent years begun to make itself strongly felt; especially it has become very marked during and since the Great War. In all our modern nations, society is stratified; it contains, not castes, but social strata which shade imperceptibly into one another. Individuals and families rise and fall freely in the social scale; nevertheless the various strata have certain standards of living, standards of comfort, of refinement, and of culture, which the members of each stratum endeavor to preserve, to live up to. Within this whole range of social strata, the broadest and most important distinction is that between the hand-workers and the brain-work-ers. Thirty and even twenty years ago, the dis-tinction was fairly sharp, sharper perhaps in Europe than in America; the strata of brain-workers made up the white-collar class or middle classes. They were expected to have, and in the main did have, a higher standard of education, of refinement, and of culture than the hand-workers. They were able to maintain this higher standard, because in the main they en-joyed a higher standard of remuneration. They endeavored especially to secure for their children a fuller education than that with which the bulk of the hand-workers were content. And they secured this fuller education for their children by expending a part of their earnings upon it.

This class, in spite of all the criticism to which it has been subjected, was of high value to the nations. Since any boy, born in the hand-working class, who showed more than average capacity, initiative, and energy, could rise into it, and since he was generally encouraged to strive to do so, it was constantly recruited by the pick of the hand-working class. The average level of culture of this class was perhaps not very high; yet it did interest itself in its self-culture, took a pride in keeping up its standards, and was a main support of all the intellectual life of the nation. Fifty years ago, it was the predominating power in the political sphere. All this was true perhaps of Great Britain in higher degree than of any other country. Yet in America the class existed and comprized a large part of the old American stock.

If this middle class had used its power selfishly, it could have preserved and increased it and maintained its privileges. But, under the influence of Universal Ethics, it has abdicated in favor of the more numerous hand-working class. The principal incidents of this abdication were, in England, the successive extensions of the political franchise. In America, the enfranchisement of all immigrants, upon their request, has played a similar leading part. But in a hundred other ways the middle class contributed to bring about the change which is now so far advanced and which, as I said, constitutes the abdication of the middle class from its position of political power and the resignation of its claims to standards of remuneration, refinement, and culture, higher than those of the mass of hand-workers. These many ways are all comprized under the general

head of efforts to level up the standards of all
classes, efforts which have been in large measure
successful. A very important element in this
process has been the moral and political support,
given by the middle class to the hand-working
classes, in the establishment of trade-unions
and in all the other modes of combined action by
means of which the latter have raised their standard of wages and of comfort.

The most striking result of all this activity is
the effect upon the relative scales of remuneration
of the two classes concerned. The wages of the
hand-working class have risen rapidly, inevitably
producing for all classes a great rise in the cost
of living. The salaries of the brain-working
class have not risen proportionally; in many cases,
perhaps the great majority, they have hardly
risen appreciably. In consequence, the mid-
dle-class incomes are no longer superior to
those of the hand-working class; and in very
many cases are far below them. The change is
most striking when we compare the incomes of
the higher strata of each of the two classes.

The higher ranks of hand-workers command
incomes far beyond the reach of most professional men, whose callings require long and

costly education and special capacity. The
average salary of ministers of religion in this
country is said to be "much less than $1,000"[1];
and it has remained unchanged, while the cost
of living has risen very greatly and the hand-
laborer's wages have risen to a degree which,
in spite of the increased price of commodities,
gave him "an increase in purchasing power of
over 35 per cent."[2] in 1922, as compared with
his pre-war condition. Wages of job pressmen
were $2,135 a year in 1921. The average wage
paid by the United States Steel Corporation
reached in 1919 the figure of $1,905; that re-
ceived by railway operatives reached $1,505
for shortened hours of labor. But the wages of
the higher strata of hand-labor, such as drivers
of railway locomotives, came very near the $5,000
mark. At the same time, full college professors
were receiving salaries averaging about half that
sum; medical practitioners who earned as much
were few and far between; and ministers of
religion earned an average salary of $735. In
the year 1919 plasterers were paid $7.25 for an

[1] J. Corbin, "The Return of the Middle Class," p. 141. N. Y.,
1922.
[2] *Ibid.*, p. 143.

eight hour day, and first lieutenants in the army only $6.97 a day.[1]

A similar state of affairs obtained in England in the first years after the war and still, in great measure, persists. Mr. C. F. G. Masterman (in "England after War") observes: "the

---

[1] I take these figures from J. Corbin, Op. cit., p. 101. I have recently been informed by a young man, who has had only a few months practice and training as a compositor, that he has earned as much as $180 in eight days by operating a linotype machine. This is a rather better rate than the highest salaries paid to full professors in the greatest universities of the country.

While these pages are in the press, the newspapers announce that the bricklayers of America have won their strike for a basic wage of $12 a day. It is added that many of them are dissatisfied with this result, because they have been accustomed to earning $18 a day. It is announced at the same time that two bacteriologists have applied for admission to the school of brick-laying; and that in New Hampshire two young men have claimed public assistance rather than accept a wage of $6 a day with board and lodging for work in the hayfields. In comparing the wages of 'white-collar' workers with those of hand-workers, it should be borne in mind that the work of the latter is in very many, probably a great majority of instances, more healthy and enjoyable and less exacting than that of the former class. We hear much of the hardships of the manual workers; and it seems to be the common assumption of social reformers that work is an evil, and that a prime aim of all social reform should be the reduction of the hours of daily labor to the smallest possible number. This is a fundamental fallacy. Few men can be reasonably happy without regular work that fills the greater part of each day. I have been assured by a very intelligent man, who has spent several years as a factory-worker but who more recently has held a responsible 'white-collar' position, that he looks back on his years of manual labor with regret and that most of his fellow-workers in the factory enjoyed their hours of labor no less than he did.

municipality pays its scavengers and street cleaners substantially higher salaries than it pays to its elementary school-teachers. No unskilled Trade Unionist would be allowed for a day to accept the salary of an average clergyman or minister of religion. In the great newspaper offices, the linotype compositor who prints the paper can afford to despise the income of the journalist who writes the paper. The general decrease in the real income of the Middle Class has been accompanied by such a complete substitution of another class as to make the double indignity even harder to endure." Again: "The real income, with present prices, of the teaching community is a scandal and a shame to a civilized State. . . . What hope is there for the future of a nation which holds out to any careful parent twice the inducement to put his child into the career of coal porterage rather than into the career of teaching?" Mr. Masterman has not altogether refrained from the familiar supercilious criticism of the dwellers in Suburbia; but it is a matter for congratulation that here at last is evidence that one man who has held an important government office is not completely blind to the most fundamental conditions of national welfare. Writing of the ridicule which has been the accustomed portion of the Middle Class, he says: "Four years of furious fighting has silenced that ridicule for ever. The London clerks, the "pals" battalions of the big towns, all "Middle Class" regiments, have been tested and found true in the ultimate experiences of human tenacity and courage. No class has more distinguished itself for re-sourcefulness, endurance and determination in war. One may smile, perhaps, at the appeal to the Government to encourage propagation from "respectable" classes living on the margin of subsistence in the suburbs, rather than from other more doubtfully "respectable" classes living on the margin of subsistence in the slums. Yet, broadly speaking, the children of the Mid-dle Class once provided the richest inheritance of the community. Its increasing sterility, however necessary under present conditions, is causing a substantial loss to the nation as well as a tragedy amongst individual lives. From these suburban centers the State should be able to draw continual supplies of fresh and vigorous young life. It does not do so . . . the "only child" or "only son," which was before the war the sole luxury permitted to so many of those black-coated anchorites, has perished in the ultimate and fierce demands of war."

The facts cited in the foregoing paragraphs illustrate a general tendency and result of the unqualified acceptance of the extreme democratic principle dictated by Universal Ethics. The tendency is, by giving predominant political power to the hand-workers, to produce a state of society in which the hand-workers, their vastly preponderant numbers efficiently organized as a fighting machine, use this preponderant power for a single purpose, the raising of their wages and the diminution of their hours of work, treating the brain-workers, the *bourgeousie*, as their natural enemies, whose work is of no value to the community and whose claims to the pursuit of happiness may justly be disregarded.

We have seen the principles of pure democracy carried to and beyond their limit by the Bolsheviki of Russia, in the wholesale slaughter of the brain-working class and the crushing of the remnant to the point of extreme misery. This is an instance in which the impetus of the movement prompted by the Universal Ethics has carried it beyond its natural logical goal. But, nevertheless, it exemplifies the tendency and the logical and natural goal of the Universal Ethics, expressing itself politically in pure or unmitigated democracy, namely the destruction of all those prerogatives which the brain-workers have enjoyed in every flourishing civilization and which, I submit, are essential to such flourishing.

For consider the inevitable consequences of such deprivation, under two heads. First, in the past the brain-workers' prerogative of better pay and better social status has excited, in every member of the hand-working class who was conscious of possessing more than ordinary capacities, the natural ambition to rise into the brain-working class, in order to secure the amenities and especially the social consideration enjoyed by that class. And this has secured to that class a constant stream of recruits consisting of the ablest members of the hand-working class. Thus, so long as these prerogatives are maintained, Society secures the maximum amount of effective brain-work from its most capable members. But, when these prerogatives are withdrawn, a main incentive to choose the more exacting life of the brain-worker ceases to operate, and the indolence natural to the greater part of mankind will inevitably bring it about that the higher capacities of very many members of Society will remain latent, undeveloped, virtually wasted.[1]

In this connection, it is important to realize that the cultivation of superior intellectual capacities is the most profitable of all undertakings for the individual and for Society; that the neglect to cultivate them is accordingly the most serious form of waste. This is true, even if we consider waste and wealth from the most narrow economic standpoint of material prosperity alone.

For the cultivation of intellect is the only field of industry in which the law of diminishing returns does not hold good. In this field indeed the law seems to be inverted, to be replaced by a law of increasing returns. Two children, two brothers let us say, are born with unequal natural abilities. The one, B, is by nature or heredity endowed with average or ordinary intellectual capacity (*i.e.*, potentiality of intellectual development); the other, A, with rather

[1] We may expect that all our bacteriologists will become bricklayers.

better capacities or intellectual potentiality. If both live in a pure democracy and both receive similar education and both remain hand-workers, and especially if they work under a trade-union system that forbids A to excel his brother in output of work, their careers will be very similar and the potential superiority of A will remain latent. Their friends may recognize that A is a little smarter than B, and allege perhaps that he might have done great things. On the other hand, if they live in a Society that offers rewards to intellectual achievement, in the form of higher pay and greater social consideration, A may respond to these incentives. At an early age he becomes ambitious to distinguish himself; he works hard at school, improving his capacities to the fullest degree and storing up knowledge and skill in the use of it; passing into college, he continues this process still more intensively. Then he enters upon a strenuous career in an intellectual profession that keeps his intellectual powers always on the strain, and brings constantly fresh gains of power and knowledge. In this way—if his constitution is so tough that he does not break down prematurely, as so many do—

he takes his place in the ranks of the accomplished brain-workers, a man who, as a scientific worker, a judge, a physician, or a great teacher, performs services to Society vastly out of proportion to the scant remuneration he earns. The potential difference between B and A, almost too small to be discernible to their fellows, has become the vast difference between an ordinary mind and a great intellect. [1]

Consider the second way in which the depression of the economic status of the brain-worker proves costly to the nation. This second effect is already strongly operative and is more serious than the former; for, while the former is merely wasteful, this second effect is positively destructive of the nation's most valuable assets, namely the *strains* of superior ability comprized in the population.

[1] It is not sufficiently realized that a high civilization, with its demands for men of special capacity and training and its various departments of specialized instrumental knowledge and skill, differentiates men more widely than any more simple state of society can do, accentuating their natural differences of capacity by the processes of education. Education is not a leveling process; it is rather a differentiating process, as we see from the illustrative example in the text. This remains true even in America, where education has been organized on the assumption that all men are of equal native capacity, and where, consequently, it fails to differentiate as fully as it should do, failing to develop to the highest degree the powers of those who are most highly gifted by nature.

Here we must consider a biological truth which is fatally imcompatible with the principles and practice of ultra-democracy.[1] This truth is that, not the individual man or woman, but rather the family is the true social unit, the family, not merely as it exists at any one moment of time, but as an organism that endures throughout an indefinite number of generations.

The family is the meeting-place of various hereditary strains; it is the means by which they are perpetuated and projected into the future. A nation, biologically regarded, is not a mere mass of coexisting individuals. It is rather a vast and enduring tissue or network of hereditary strains, complexly interwoven throughout the past and constantly becoming woven into fresh combinations. The strains or strands of this tissue are of unequal value; some are strong, some are weak in very various degrees. Of this network families are the nodal points, from which the living strands are pro-

---

[1] In my lectures I used the expression "unmitigated democracy." This accurately describes the extreme form of democracy that recognizes no inequalities of natural endowment or of qualification for leadership. But the word "unmitigated" is liable to be regarded as dyslogistic and question-begging. I therefore use in place of it the term "ultra-democracy."

jected in fresh combinations. Any strand, no matter how strong, can maintain itself only a little while. If it does not, within the brief space of some forty years, enter by fertile marriage into a new node or family, its career is finished for all time. At the nodal points, the strains or threads of various values or strengths come into new combinations. Where strong threads are woven together, a strong strand results; where weak threads are woven together, feeble strands result. Where strong and weak come together, the resulting strands are of various values, but on the whole are of intermediate strength.

In every society, in every nation, multitudes of these threads or strains fail to make contact at new nodes, and thus come to an end. Their place is taken by new strands formed at the nodes. Thus the texture of the whole fabric woven on the loom of time, although it is continuous through indefinite periods, is subject to change of quality. If, in each unit-period, in each generation, the strong and the weak threads, the threads of various values, make the nodal contacts in equal proportions, the strength of the fabric remains unchanged. If the stronger threads make the nodal contacts in greater proportion than the weaker, the fabric becomes stronger and stronger. If the stronger threads fail to make their contacts in equal proportion with the weaker ones, the whole fabric deteriorates in strength and quality.

Such changes may take place very rapidly, as viewed in the long perpective of history. When social conditions within a nation are such as to favor the nodal contacts of the stronger strains, we see the great periods of intense national activity and achievement, such as the great ages of Greece and Rome, the Elizabethan and the Victorian period in England, the post-revolutionary period of the United States of America. When conditions in any nation are favorable to the perpetuation of the weaker strains and unfavorable to that of the stronger, we see the periods of stagnation or decay.

Now the conditions we have been considering, as the inevitable outcome of ultra-democracy, are conditions of this latter kind. They are conditions unfavorable to the perpetuation of the stronger strains or threads. In other words, under those conditions the brain-working class, formed by the rise into it of the more capable strains of the hand-working class through many generations, becomes relatively infertile; within it, celibacy, late marriage, and the severely restricted family become the rule, while the fertility of the hand-working class is encouraged, and maintains itself or actually increases.

Thus within the nation the principles of Universal Ethics, bringing about the regime of ultra-democracy, tend to produce on the small scale and are now actually producing within many, perhaps all, of the modern nations, that deplorable effect which they tend to produce and are producing on the world-wide scale, namely the progressive supplanting of the stronger strains by the weaker, of the more finely constituted by the more grossly constituted.[1]

[1] Russia is not the only country in which the middle class is being exterminated so rapidly that the process forces itself on the attention of every observer. Thus Mr. Langdon Mitchell after a visit to Germany in 1922, writes (*Atlantic Monthly*, April, 1923) of "one sinister phenomenon that impressed me most—the fall of the middle class. There was painful evidence of the decay of that class, on all sides. . . . The professional class, which creates and sustains civilization, is being rapidly abolished. It needs no Trotzky or Radek to destroy it; the tyranny of circumstance suffices . . . the scholarship, science, medicine, and art of Central Europe are actually disappearing." And, he adds, the result must be that "the people that produced Luther, must necessarily perish as a creative force. That is, their civilization will cease to exist. But, civilization once

It is perhaps worth while to repeat the argument in brief in the following condensed form. The universal individualist ethics, carried to its logical conclusion, demands that the whole of mankind form one society, without national boundaries and without racial distinctions. And it requires that this vast society shall be organized on the principles of communism. All men shall share equally in the fruits of the earth and in the products of human thought and human labor. Suppose this state of affairs to be established and maintained, every man practising faithfully the principles of strict com-

---

rooted out and gone, cannot be wished back into being. There is a dream among men that it is not so. We think of Civilization as of the Earth or Air: it cannot conceivably suffer diminution, or be absent, but it must be recalled that modern science and its child, modern civilization, or progress, are not like the Roman state and culture, robust and enduring things, iron and granite, which only time and erosion can destroy: they are as frail as any weed, and yet more frail. For they depend on money; on a class of highly bred human animals with well-trained minds; on a degree of leisure in that class; and on a selfless enthusiasm. Let the educated men and women of a community become hewers of wood and drawers of water—all is over; the thing ends; you have a dark age."

Mr. John Corbin ("The Return of the Middle Class") has shown that the same process is going on more slowly and subtly in America. And in Great Britain, there is good reason to believe, the same influences are working towards the same end only rather less effectively than in Germany. Cf. C. F. G. Masterman "England after the War" and "England?" by an Overseas Englishman.

munism and of brotherly love, always post-
poning his own claims and interests to those of
his fellow men. If we make this impossible
supposition, we shall see that in this earthly
paradise there would prevail a differential
reproduction-rate.

The disciplined energies of all mankind being
bent upon providing the material basis of universal comfort, on banishing disease and keeping down the death-rate to the minimum, and
on providing pleasurable recreations for the
masses, the masses would respond by raising
their birth-rate to a natural maximum, and
population would double itself everywhere every
twenty years or less.

The more capable and energetic individuals,
denied the incentives of family and national
sentiment and of personal distinction, would
cease to put forth the abundant energies and
powers which vitalize our civilization and are
the source of all wealth,[1] all culture and all
progress. And especially, these individuals,
looking into the future and seeing no prospect
for themselves and their like, beyond the perpetual struggle to maintain a reasonable stand-

[1] I use "wealth" here in the literal sense as the opposite of "poverty."

ard of physical comfort for the ever-increasing
hordes of population, as they press with increasing urgency upon the means of subsistence,
the common stock of human resources, these
individuals would be content to do their communistic duty and to pass away, without
perpetuating their strains. The prevalence
throughout a brief period of such differential
reproduction would exterminate all higher aspirations; it would produce throughout the world a
population that would spend all of its leisure
jigging to the jolly strains of jazz-bands, gazing
at sensational trivial 'movies', and applauding
the heroes of the milder forms of gladiatorial
combat. After a brief space of time, the Fatty
Arbuckles, the Charlie Chaplins, the Babe
Ruths, and the Queens of the Musical Revue
would reign supreme as the beneficent dis-
pensers of the preferred pleasures of the populace.

Such would be the result of the universal practice of Universal Ethics. And the result would
be the same, even if science should shortly
discover and put at our disposal immense
new sources of energy (such as the internal
energy of the atom) and should teach us to

synthesize food from the elements or otherwise to produce it in unlimited quantities. Population could then multiply itself on the earth many times. The theoretical limit of population would be very far away in the future. For all practical purposes we might regard the number of mankind as subject to no limit; yet even then, I say, swift decadence would be the inevitable result of Universal Ethics ruthlessly applied.

But we have no guarantee that any such discoveries can be made. They are in fact highly improbable. And, if they are beyond our power to achieve, we have to reckon with the continued sway of the most fundamental law of human life, namely, that the multiplication of every community and of the whole population of the world always has been and always will be limited by the supply of the means of subsistence, or broadly by the available supply of food and energy.

Until the opening of the 19th century, the population of the various regions of the earth had remained stationary for long ages, or had on the whole very slowly increased, with more rapid increases and decreases of purely local and temporary character. Then came the dis-

covery of the means of tapping and harnessing
the great reserves of stored energy, first coal
and then oil. This, by vastly facilitating
mechanical transportation, brought all the surface of the earth within easy reach and so extended greatly the sources of food-supply. In
consequence, population multiplied as it had
never done before and as, in all probability, it
never can do again.

We are nearing the close of this great period
of rapid multiplication, based on the intensive
mechanical exploitation of the earth's reserves
of energy and of fertile soil. During that period
we have become accustomed to the altogether
abnormal and unique condition of almost unlimited multiplication of the human race. We
have come to assume that such rapid multiplication is the normal or natural state of affairs,
and that it will and must continue indefinitely.
But that is a gross error. We are, as I said,
nearing the close of that great and unique
period. Mankind has now to return and to adjust its customs to something like the old order
of things, namely, an approximately stationary
population. Once more, as throughout the ages
preceding the 19th century, the enormous po-

tential fecundity of mankind must be severely limited.[1]

The natural fecundity or multiplication-rate has been approached by any population only here and there, under the most favorable conditions and for brief periods, as in the colonial days of America. Let us clearly understand this fact—its realization would mean that every woman would bear and rear on the average at least ten children. The exercise of the reproductive function has, then, to be very severely limited; and it will be so limited through the long ages that stretch before us. The practice of Universal Ethics would mean that everywhere the function would be exercised chiefly by the most primitive, the least civilized, the least cultured, the least assimilable members of every community, and that everywhere the higher types of mankind would exercise increasingly, in one way or another, a severe self-restraint in respect of this function.

The prevalence of that state of affairs throughout a brief period would suffice to destroy all the institutions, undermine all the traditions,

---

[1] Cf. Prof. E. M. East's "Mankind at the Crossroads," a book which shows how near we live to the margin of subsistence.

and degrade all the moral, intellectual, and æsthetic standards of our civilization.

It may be said, there is little danger that the precepts of Universal Ethics shall be generally acted upon. I reply that, even though not generally acted upon, their acceptance as the sole acknowledged moral basis of our civilization constitutes a very serious danger and that, in so far as they influence the conduct of men, they must tend to produce the deplorable results I have indicated; further, that they have already exerted a very considerable effect of this kind.

Thus on the large world-wide scale, as on the smaller national scale, the principles of Universal Ethics, when they begin effectively to control the relations of peoples and the social relations and conditions within the nations, inevitably make for the deterioration both of the living fabric which is the human race and of the spiritual fabric which is civilization. They threaten thus to bring to an end the progress of mankind. And the progress of civilization is threatened not merely with stagnation upon the mediocre level already achieved. It is only too probable that, with the slowing down of all higher forms of activity and the acceptance of progressively lower standards in all the works of taste and intellect, the ascending process must be converted into one of actual retrocession and decay.

This is a gloomy picture. But I have not drawn it as a forecaste of what must inevitably happen. I say it expresses a tendency which will more and more realize itself, if we do not boldly think through the moral problem confronting our civilization and achieve the needed synthesis of National with Universal Ethics.

LECTURE V

A Synthesis of National with Universal Ethics is the Need of Our Time

I HAVE sketched very briefly the argument
which shows that the principles of Universal
Ethics are in themselves inadequate to secure the
higher interests of mankind and that they must,
if strictly applied, prove fatal to those interests.
I believe my reasoning is capable of being sub-
stantiated in detail and at length, such as I
cannot attempt in this brief course of lectures.
I must be content to have demonstrated that the
present conditions of the world and especially
two factors, the immensely increased facility of
transportation and the control of the death-rate,
force upon our consideration problems and
probabilities that were entirely beyond the ken
of earlier ages.

The moral philosophers have envisaged their
problems without considering the immense com-
plication introduced by the tendencies of popu-

lation we have briefly considered. In the main, the vision of each has been restricted to his own people. This is most obviously true of those who have taught a national ethics; but it has been hardly less true of those who have taught a universal system. The fact was amusingly illustrated by the great Greek philosophers, who, though they claimed to seek ethical principles of universal validity, yet failed to take into their ethical purview even the slaves that dwelt among them and the barbarians that pressed upon their frontiers.

In the main the vision of modern philosophers has been hardly more wide-ranging. The few exponents of National Ethics have had in view the citizens of their own State. Fichte and Hegel, for example, conceived their moral philosophy on behalf of the Prussian State and for the guidance or control of the citizens of that State.

The modern exponents of Universal Ethics have professed to lay down the principles of conduct for all men; but they have been content to assume that the men they knew most familiarly, the best of their fellow citizens, were a fair sample of all mankind; and they have neglected to consider the consequences for the world in general of the universal practice of their principles. But I am not the first to discern the tendency of the Universal Ethics, though I am endeavoring to define it more broadly and explicitly than has been done before. Others have discerned this essential incompatibility between Universal Ethics and human progress; and it has filled them with something like consternation or despair. I will refer to only one thinker as illustrating this effect.[1] T. H. Huxley devoted the best part of his life to the study and exposition of the principles of biological evolution. In his old age he turned to ponder problems of human destiny; then he glimpsed the great antagonism I speak of. And in his famous Romanes lecture he set forth in eloquent and impressive language this disharmony (as it seemed to him) between "Evolution and Ethics."

Huxley, like many others since the publication of "The Origin of Species," saw that the ethical restraints of civilization tend to reduce to a minimum the operation of natural selection

[1] Friederich Nietzsche's philosophy may, I think, be said to be his reaction to the perception of the destructive tendency of Universal Ethics. In the violence of his reaction he poured out the child with the bath-water and preached an ethics that was neither national nor universal, but purely individual and aristocratic.

upon the human race; and, since he believed that natural selection alone had evolved the higher qualities of the race and was essential for their continued maintenance, he spoke of an inevitable opposition between the ethical and the cosmic processes. He wrote: "I have termed this evolution of the feelings out of which the primitive bonds of human society are so largely forged, into the organized and personified sympathy we call conscience, the ethical process. So far as it tends to make any human society more efficient in the struggle for existence with the state of nature, or with other societies, it works in harmonious contrast with the cosmic process. But it is none the less true that, since law and morals are restraints upon the struggle for existence between men in society, the ethical process is in opposition to the principle of the cosmic process, and tends to the suppression of the qualities best fitted for success in that struggle.

"It is further to be observed that, just as the self-assertion, necessary to the maintenance of society against the state of nature, will destroy that society if it is allowed free operation within; so the self-restraint, the essence of the ethical process, which is no less an essential condition of the existence of every polity, may, by excess, become ruinous to it."[1]

And, writing of the logical consequence of Universal Ethics, he said—"It is desirable to recognize the fact that these consequences are incompatible with the existence of a civil state, under any circumstances of this world which have obtained, or, so far as one can see, are likely to come to pass."[2]

In view of this opposition between the cosmic process of evolution and the ethical process of increasingly effective self-restraint, he despaired of bringing "the course of evolution into harmony with even the elementary requirements of the ethical ideal of the just and the good."[3] And he wrote: "Thus, brought before the tribunal of ethics, the cosmos might well seem to stand condemned." And again: "Cosmic nature is no school of virtue, but the headquarters of the enemy of ethical nature" and "the cosmos works through the lower nature of man, not for righteousness, but against it."[4]

---

[1] "Collected Essays" by T. H. Huxley, Vol. IX, p. 31.
[2] Op. Cit., p. 32.   [3] Op. Cit., p. 58.
[4] Op. Cit., p. 76.

"By the Tiber, as by the Ganges, ethical man admits that the cosmos is too strong for him; and, destroying every bond which ties him to it, by ascetic discipline, he seeks salvation in absolute renunciation. Modern thought is making a fresh start from the base whence Indian and Greek philosophy set out; and, the human mind being very much what it was five-and-twenty centuries ago, there is no ground for wonder if it presents indications of a tendency to move along the old lines to the same results." [1]

Huxley concluded by saying, "Let us understand, once for all, that the ethical progress of society depends, not on imitating the cosmic process, still less in running away from it, but in combating it."

This is, as he said, "an audacious proposal"; and, if we have to accept Huxley's view that the ethical and the cosmic processes are necessarily and forever in conflict, and that we are compelled by our ethical principles to combat the cosmic process, then, I am afraid, the combat must be for us a hopelessly unequal struggle in which we shall be worsted; then, in truth, it remains only to choose between the pessimistic

[1] Op. Cit., p. 78.

resignation of the Stoic and the pietistic resignation of the mystic ascetic who looks to a world we know not of, to offset the incurable evils of the world we know.

I venture to suggest that Huxley's conclusion is not well founded; that it can be bettered. If the ethical process is, as Huxley held and as I hold, an outcome of the cosmic process, how can the two processes be essentially in conflict? And if the former undertake to combat its progenitor, how can it hope for success?

May it not be that this conflict between the ethical and the cosmic processes is a false appearance, an illusion produced by a false conception of the ethical process, by inadequate conception of ethical principles. Throughout his discussion Huxley assumed that the ethical process is necessarily governed by the principles of Universal Ethics. He never paused to consider whether the principles of National Ethics may not also have a certain validity, and whether, by recognizing such validity, we may not achieve ethical principles by aid of which we may reconcile the ethical process with the cosmic process of evolution. That we may hope to do this is the essential suggestion I wish to make.

I suggest that our task, as moral agents, is, not to enter into futile hopeless combat against the cosmic process, but rather to revise our conception of the ethical process and to achieve ethical principles which will enable us, while coöperating with the cosmic process, to guide it, modify it, moralize it, and at the same time accelerate it.

If we are right in believing that the cosmic process has slowly evolved the intellectual and moral nature of man as its highest product, Huxley's proposal to combat that process is not only audacious, it is also in the last degree rash and unwise, or, in short, unethical.

When in 1893 I first read Huxley's famous Romanes Lecture in the pages of the London *Times* on the morrow of its delivery, I received a severe moral shock followed by a profound depression. From that shock and depression I have never wholly recovered. These present lectures are my delayed reaction to the shock; in them I am endeavoring to work my way out of the pessimistic impasse in which, as it seemed, Huxley's lecture left us.

I begin, then, the constructive section of these lectures by insisting that it is the essential

nature and function of Mind to exert a progressively intelligent, foresighted, purposeful
guidance upon the seemingly blind mechanical
processes of the material world, including those
processes of natural selection which seem to have
played so great a part hitherto in fashioning
the nature and destiny of mankind.

If Mind has this power of guidance, it may
hope to guide, though it may not effectively
combat, the cosmic process. For it follows that
man's moral nature is not a principle alien to
the cosmic process; his conscience is not an
unnatural power that impels him for all time
to fight a hopeless and losing battle against
the forces of Nature. That is a view of morality
to which we are led, if we start out with any intuitive theory of moral conduct, if we repudiate
the Utilitarian principle.

For, if we reject the Utilitarian principle, believing that our moral ideal is fixed for us by
some supernatural moral organ or faculty, and
that we cannot modify our notions of what is
right and wrong in the light of experience of
the consequences of conduct, then our moral
ideal must be static, incapable of development or evolution; and we naturally are con-

demned to follow the universal and individualist ethics.

The immediate prompting of our nature leads us directly to approve such precepts as the universal systems have set forth—that we always turn the other cheek to the smiter: that we always and everywhere subordinate our own welfare, and that of those nearest us, to the welfare of those who are further from us: [1] that we regard all men as created equal and as of equal value: that every man shall be treated only as an end in himself and never as a means: that all men have an equal claim to an equal share of all that is worth having. And, if it can be clearly shown, as I have endeavored to show you in the foregoing lectures, that any such system, literally carried into universal practise, must quickly bring civilization to an end and plunge mankind back into depths of barbaric disorder, with consequent vast suffer-

[1] The reader may question this statement; but it is, I believe, generally true of persons of rare and extreme generosity. Such persons identify themselves so closely with those to whom they are personally attached that they include them in their sphere of self-sacrifice, or rather tend to postpone the interest of these loved ones, together with their own, to those of the stranger without the gates. And this tendency though it rarely, if ever, determines the actions of most of us, does, I believe, work obscurely in many men and in more women.

ing to many millions, still the principles of intuitive morals require us to continue on this destructive path, heroically practising the accepted principles, while we witness and share in the chaos they are producing; they require us, as Huxley said, to continue what we (falsely) conceive to be the ethical endeavor hopelessly to combat the cosmic process. Or, alternatively, we might regard ourselves as condemned to a merely stoical contemplation of the cosmic process, as determinist philosophers would have us believe. But if we were, in fact, compelled by logic or philosophy to accept the determinist view of the cosmic process, a lofty scorn for its inanities, such as Mr. B. Russell proposes to us,[1] would be for most of us but a poor and ineffective antidote to the distress which the contemplation of it must engender.

On the other hand, if we recognize the truth that we are part of the cosmic process, not passively enduring parts, but rather the growing points of the evolutionary process, the parts in which the creative energy of Life and Mind finds its fullest expression, parts in which intelligent purpose is beginning to take a vastly

[1] "A Free Man's Religion."

wider scope than it has done in the past, then we see that it is our highest task, not to define some statical ethical formula, fixed for all time by some unnatural or supernatural principle, and to deduce from it the rules of conduct, but rather to discover, by the aid of all our vast and increasing stores of knowledge, how we best may coöperate in the cosmic process, so guiding it as to carry to yet higher levels that highest product of evolution, the cultured life of well-organized societies, societies in which alone human nature can realize its higher potentialities.

If we find that what we have assumed to be the essential principles of ethics must lead the human race to disaster and degradation, our duty is, not to exclaim "*fiat justitia, ruat cœlum,*" but rather to re-examine our ethical assumptions in the light of the consequences to which they lead, and, if necessary, to revise and amend them according to the Utilitarian principle.

In making this revision, we have to assume a responsibility which moral philosophers have never yet recognized.[1] They have been content to take Man for granted, to accept human

---

[1] Nietzsche and Spencer were partial exceptions.

nature as a fixed quality, and to reason about, and to legislate for, the standard moral man; as the economists of the last century reasoned about a standard economic man. The new task, the new responsibility, of scientific ethics is to decide, not only how men should act, but also what they should be; to determine, not only how human nature, being what it is, should conduct itself, but also what kind of human nature is most desirable, what type of man is to prevail increasingly in numbers throughout the earth: in short, ethics can no longer be content to seek and to formulate the ideal of conduct for human nature as it is; it must also assume the responsibility of formulating an ideal of human nature as it may come to be.

The first step towards the new ethical synthesis must be the frank realization that Ethics cannot be divorced from Politics. Such divorce has been the fatal error of the philosophers who have taught the Universal Ethics. Yet some great thinkers have seen this truth. Long ago Plato embodied his principal ethical teaching in the book ("The Republic") in which he sketched the political organization of his ideal State, recognizing no separation between the principles of Ethics and of Politics. And in a later age, another great thinker, Edmund Burke, explicitly announced the same truth, declaring that "the principles of true politics are but those of morals enlarged."

Even if Ethics and Politics are regarded merely as sciences which enquire into the existing order of things, seeking to describe that order and to explain how it has come about, they cannot properly be treated as distinct and independent studies. And, when they are conceived as philosophy, as enquiries into what ought to be, rather than into what actually is and has been, then they are, or should be, intimate and inseparable aspects of one enquiry. For, when we set out to enquire—What is the true goal of human purpose and endeavor? we cannot treat of man as an individual merely. We see at once that our enquiry concerns, not the isolated individual man (that pale abstraction with which psychology has too exclusively dealt) but the concrete men and women whose lives are but a part of the life of an organic whole, the life of organized society, from participation in which the individual acquires whatever value or importance he may have. We see that the worth

of his purposes, of his ideals, and of his efforts
to realize them, must be judged with reference
to their effects upon the life of Society. We see
also that, in turn, political ideals must be
evaluated with reference to their effects upon
the lives of individual men now existing; and that,
more importantly, they must be judged also
with reference to the lives of the generations
yet unborn, and especially with reference to
the qualities of the men of those future
generations.

We have, then, to ask, not only—How should
men act and live? but also—What manner of
man is best fitted to the best life? And we cannot answer these questions in any deeper sense,
without asking also—How should Society be
organized, in order that the best men may
exist and realize the best life?

The separation of these two great questions, the
ethical and the political, the attempt to answer
either one without at the same time considering
the other, has been the ground of the sterility
of much ethical and political discussion. It
is the fundamental error of the Universal Ethics,
as well as of the extreme forms of National
Ethics, such as the Machiavellian and the

Hegelian. And this separation has prevented us from achieving the much needed synthesis of National with Universal Ethics, to replace the unstable and perplexing compromises which hitherto have served as the moral basis of our western civilization.

Recognizing, then, that ethical and political principles and precepts are not eternal truths which we can discover by deduction from moral axioms of any kind, or by listening to the pronouncements of some mysterious supernatural voice or organ within us, some divinely implanted moral faculty, a "moral sense" or "conscience," but that they are rather means towards a goal; we must define that goal as clearly as possible, in order that we may choose, and may refine by critical examination, the ethico-political principles which will best further the progress of mankind toward that goal.

Surveying the various goals proposed by the ultilitarian philosophers of the past, we find that two such goals claim our allegiance above all others, in virtue both of their intrinsic reasonableness and of the weight of philosophic opinion by which each is maintained. One is "the greatest happiness of the greatest number," the greatest possible happiness of all human beings dwelling on the earth. The other is the development to the highest possible degree of the potential capacities of the human race, of the species Homo Sapiens, or, in other words, the finest possible flowering of all that we call human culture and the higher life of man.

The former is the goal proposed by those philosophers of the Utilitarian School who vitiated their system by making the false doctrine of psychological hedonism a part of it. They are the group to whom the term "utilitarian" is commonly applied and who openly avow the utilitarian principles. Bentham was the most prominent and thorough exponent of the principles of this group. They may be called the pleasure-Utilitarians. Those who have proposed the other goal have not usually acknowledged the utilitarian principle. For they have been averse from being confounded with the pleasure-Utilitarians. And they have been accustomed to claim that the use of the term "higher," in their formulation of the goal of human endeavor, excludes them from the utilitarian class. And, in a similar way, it has often been asserted that J. S. Mill, in recognizing the distinction between what he called higher and lower pleasures, implicitly transcended the utilitarian principles. For it is said that the comparative valuation implied by the word "higher" is only to be achieved by means of an intuitive function, and that therefore any ethical system which recognizes higher and lower goals of action is essentially an intuitional rather than a utilitarian system. This is merely a confusion that arises from bad psychology. Let us recognize, then, that both the "greatest happiness" principle and the "highest culture" principle are utilitarian in the broad and proper sense of the word; and let us admit that they both have very strong claims for acceptance.

We have next to ask—Are these two principles opposed to one another, as they have commonly been represented to be? May it not be possible to formulate our goal in a way which will reconcile and synthesize these two seemingly opposed ideals?

I suggest at once that such synthesis is possible and may be indicated in a single brief formula, namely—the highest happiness of the greatest number. But this formula requires further interpretation. The phrase "the greatest number" is ambiguous. Does it mean the greatest possible number of those living at the present moment and in the immediate future? Or does it mean "the greatest number" in the long run? That is to say, in formulating our goal or ideal, must we have regard only to our contemporaries and our immediate descendants? Or should we have regard also to the generations of the remote future? Clearly, the latter.[1]

---

[1] It is the most serious ambiguity and defect of almost all statements of the utilitarian principle that they do not clearly formulate or attempt to answer this fundamental question. According as one or other answer be given to it, the utilitarian principle will dictate one or other of two widely different practical policies. This ambiguity may be illustrated by a recent statement of the utilitarian principle in which this essential question is almost, though not quite, explicitly recognized. Prof. R. B. Perry (in "The Present Conflict of Ideals") writes: "We may construe utilitarianism in the broad sense to mean that right conduct is the means to human happiness" (p. 493). Further he writes: "The merit of any social system is to be judged by the happiness which it creates. And a social system may as fairly be judged by the lot of men at the bottom as by the lot of men at the top. It is comparatively easy to devise a system that shall make some men happy, provided the majority may be sacrificed for the purpose. The great task of civilization is to achieve a happiness that may be generally shared, by which the good of one man shall also balance the good of another" (p. 500). To this statement we need to add the following: It is comparatively easy to devise a system that shall make all men happy, provided that we are under no obligation to the future, that the system is required only to secure the happiness of the great majority of persons now living, and is not concerned to secure the further progress and diffusion of the higher forms of culture, nor even to provide against the universal stagnation and decay of civilization.

We cannot rationally approve of any system which would secure even the highest and greatest happiness of all existing human beings, if it were essentially unstable, if it were such as to destroy itself after a short time, giving place inevitably to some system under which the mass of mankind would be condemned to prolonged misery.

Mr. H. G. Wells, in the first and greatest of his imaginative stories,[1] has depicted for us a society which came near to realizing the ideal of "the greatest happiness of the greatest number." But we all should agree that that society of jolly little people, who spent their lives in a perpetual round of innocent, graceful, and æsthetically pleasing activities, was gravely defective in two respects. The pleasure and the happiness of the people were relatively low in the scale; and they were low in the scale, just because they were the product of a social organization which provided no guarantee for their continuance, and gave no scope and no incentive to efforts for further development.

It is probable that if, owing to some miraculous change in human nature (such as Mr. Wells

[1] "The Time Machine."

has described in "The Days of the Comet") a completely socialistic or communistic organization of society throughout the world could be rapidly and completely established, we should see an approximation to the ideal of the greatest happiness of the greatest number of the then existing human beings.

But such a system would have the two fatal defects of Mr. Wells' Society of little people. The happiness of the people would be on a relatively low level; and it would be on a low level largely because the system would inevitably be an unstable degenerating system, one containing the seeds of its own ineffectiveness and rapid decay. It would be a degenerative rather than a stable and progressive system, for the biological and psychological reasons I have already indicated; and also for a reason which has been more generally recognized; namely, it would rapidly consume all the natural resources of the earth and exhaust all the stores of capital which men have accumulated and without which civilization cannot be maintained. In other words, under such a system, consumption would soon vastly outstrip production, and the common store of good things would steadily and rapidly diminish until, though all shared alike, the share of each would be a mere pittance.

It will be commonly agreed, then, that the ideal system must have regard to the remote, as well as to the immediate, future; that we cannot be content to say "eat, drink, and be happy; posterity has done nothing for us, let posterity look out for itself"; that we cannot approve of a system which would give good results now and in the near future, if its remote results must be the decay and self-destruction of all that we call civilization.

We must, therefore, amend our formula by adding some sufficient recognition of the claims of future generations. It may then run as follows: Our goal must be the highest happiness of the greatest number enduring throughout an indefinitely prolonged future; or, more briefly —*the enduring and highest happiness of the greatest number.*

And we must refuse to regard each man only as an end in himself; we must regard him also as a means towards this goal. We must recognize, not only that each man can exercise by moral choice an intelligent direction upon his own development, but also that the human race can and must learn to exercise a similar intelligent direction of its own development, and, by doing so, progressively realize the ideal of human nature, that nature which is best suited to the attainment of the supreme ethical end, the enduring and highest happiness of the greatest number.

Accepting this as the goal of ethical endeavor, we see at once that political and social organizations are the all important means towards the realization of this goal. We see also that, in judging the value of any actual or proposed organization of society, we must attach to its stability and to its cumulative effects over long periods of time at least as much importance as we assign to it in virtue of its immediate contribution to the happiness of the greatest number.

We shall find that this formula implies that synthesis of National with Universal Ethics which, as I have already shown reason to think, is the crying need of our time.

The Universal Ethics naturally tends to express itself politically as pure democracy, what I shall speak of as ultra-democracy. Assuming that all men are of equal value, in respect both of their claims and of their powers, and that they are to be treated only as ends in themselves and not at all as means to the flourishing of the State or nation and to the welfare of future generations, ultra-democracy demands that every man shall have an equal voice in the control of public affairs. For it assumes that each man knows best what he wants and can best judge how to obtain what he wants. Hence the political formula of Universal Ethics is—to each adult one vote, or universal suffrage.

National Ethics, on the other hand, naturally tends to find political expression in an aristocratic organization of society. This for two reasons. First, regarding the welfare of the Nation as of prime importance, because an essential condition of the higher happiness of future generations, it sees that all existing members of the Nation must be treated in some considerable degree as means to this end; and it recognizes that this end, the welfare of the Nation as an organic unity that lives and moves among other similar organisms, can best be secured by placing the main responsibility for, and power of control over, the affairs of the Nation in a limited number of men specially qualified by training and by experience for the tasks of statesmanship.

Secondly, it recognizes that men are not equally endowed, but that some are by natural endowment much better qualified than others to undertake the duties of leadership and control in all public affairs. It holds that the principal purpose of political organization should be to secure that such individuals, those having the best natural endowment for the tasks of statesmanship, should be given the training, the experience, and the power that will enable them to control the destiny of the Nation.

Politically, then, the synthesis of National with Universal Ethics will demand a synthesis of the aristocratic with the democratic principle.

Such synthesis is not impossible; the democratic and the aristocratic principles are not incapable of being combined. History displays for our contemplation certain instances of nations that have achieved such synthesis in imperfect forms; and these instances, imperfect as they were, were yet, of all political organizations that the world has known, the most successful in promoting progress towards the goal we have defined—the higher happiness of the greatest number enduring through an indefinitely long period.

I would cite, as the best among such instances, Greece in its great age, the Roman Republic, England in the middle of the nineteenth century,[1] and America in the days of the founding of the Republic. In all these the synthesis of universal with national principles was only very imperfectly and partially realized; yet they remain as the high-water marks of human achievement, the times and places in which most progress was made towards the ultimate ethical goal.

[1] W. H. Lecky's deliberate judgment was that no country was ever better governed than England under the Whig aristocracy in the middle of the 19th century.

LECTURE VI

SUGGESTIONS TOWARDS THE SYNTHESIS

LET us be clear about two facts. First, that the principle of ultra-democracy, although its advocates have always taken a high moral line, claiming for all men highly developed moral capacities, is yet founded upon a deep-lying distrust of human nature. It claims that every man should have an equal voice in the control of affairs, on the ground that no man can be trusted to act fairly towards his fellowmen, that every man who may hold power in his hands will use it unjustly, that he will not act ethically, striving only to realize the ethico-political ideal, but will rather act unjustly for his own advantage. That is a very grave indictment of human nature. If it were true, the outlook would indeed be dark. The principle of ultra-democracy, then, is a counsel of despair, rooted in a dark pessimistic view of the potentialities of human nature. It is, therefore, natural that we commonly find, in the writings of its advocates, an illogical mixture of lofty moral pretensions and of cynical pessimism; a mixture that gives a tone of unreality and lack of good faith to so much of the writings of this school.

Secondly, let us be clear that the principles of ultra-democracy have never yet been practised by any large and enduring community. All the modern nations that are organized more or less democratically have adopted some form of representative democracy. And representative democracy, as rightly conceived, and as conceived by the founders of this great republic, does essentially imply and aim at the synthesis of democratic with aristocratic principles which is the true political expression of the ethical synthesis I have indicated. For representative democracy, so conceived, aims at securing, as the representatives of the people, the men best qualified by capacity and experience to guide and control the affairs of the nation; making of them, not mere delegates of their constituencies, but representatives responsible for exercising their own best judgment on all matters with which they are charged.

Thus the wisdom of statesmen has outrun the insight of moral philosophers; practice, as in so many other fields, has preceded theory; political institutions have been shaped in accordance with a moral philosophy that has not yet been formulated. For representative democracy implies, as its ethical basis, that synthesis of National with Universal Ethics which we have found to be the ethical basis necessary to our civilization.

The practical man, in face of this fact, is likely to ask—If we already have the right sort of political institutions, why trouble about the theoretical or philosophical basis? To this the answer is that the influence of Universal Ethics, explicitly accepted as the basis of democracy, has inevitably tended strongly to subvert the principle of representative democracy; chiefly in two ways: (a) by converting the representative into a mere delegate; (b) by extending unduly the basis of representation; in both cases in accordance with the implicit cynical assumptions of ultra-democracy, namely, that all men are created equal and that all men are equally unworthy to be trusted with power over their fellowmen. This subversive tendency is, I say,

inevitably the influence of the universal individualist ethics, which regards every man
solely as an end and neglects to regard the nation
as a means to the ultimate ethical goal, a means
higher and vastly more important than all the
existing men in whom at any one moment the
life of the nation is embodied.

Only by consciously accepting the nation as
such an ethical means of supreme value, that is
to say, only by embodying in our ethical basis
the truths of National Ethics as well as those of
Universal Ethics, can we hope to counteract this
subversive tendency; a tendency which is destroying representative democracy, in favor of
ultra-democracy working by the method of
delegation.

The general tendency of thinkers who, like
Huxley, have perceived the disharmony between
organic evolution of the human race and the
principles of Universal Ethics has been to em-
phasize the importance of social evolution
(including under that term all improvement of
culture as well as of social organization) and to
belittle the importance of the innate qualities
of men. They point to the fact that individuals
of almost all races have shown themselves ca-

pable of assimilating the most advanced culture and even of contributing to its further advance. And they make the inference that, if only the forms of social organization and especially the processes of education can be maintained and further improved, all will be well with our civilization, no matter what changes may occur in the native qualities of the populations which are the bearers of it. [1]

[1] Few perhaps would maintain this position, if the question were presented in some such concrete form as—Do you believe that civilization could thrive in a population consisting of morons or feeble-minded persons only? Those who profess indifference to the question of the quality and changes of quality of the population, and maintain the dogma of natural equality, presumably postulate as the substance of society a population of normal men and women, leaving out of consideration the subnormal part of the population. Yet there is only too good reason to believe that the subnormal part is already very large and rapidly increasing.

During a large part of the period of the Great War, it was my duty to survey all cases of mental and nervous break-down sent home from the British armies in all parts of the world, and to select, from among them all, such cases as I deemed suitable for treatment in open hospital wards. The task was a very distressing one for any man of normal sensibilities, although it was in a sense an errand of mercy. I am not one of those who maintain that only men of degenerate or naturally unstable constitution broke down mentally and nervously under the strain of war. My experience, of nearly five years' duration, in the handling of such cases convinced me that the best constituted man was liable to break down, if the strain were sufficiently great and prolonged. But, in addition to cases of this type, I saw, in a never-ending stream, thousands of poor unstable creatures, many of whom had suffered moral collapse as soon as, or before, they had come within sound of the guns or even without having been assigned to service abroad. Yet most of these

These thinkers see that, as Professor Hobhouse says[1]: "The factors which determine the survival of physical organisms, if applied as rules for the furtherance of social progress, appear to conflict with all that social progress means." That is to say, they see that deliberate destruction of the less fit, after the manner of natural selection, is incompatible with any ethical order of Society. And, failing to see that, under civiliza-

men had volunteered for military service, and all of them had been accepted by the medical officers whose duty it was to reject the obviously unfit among the recruits. No one, I think, could have passed through this experience without developing a grave anxiety as to the soundness of the national stock. If any American is inclined to suppose that, as regards the population of his country, there is no occasion for such anxiety, I would refer him to the statistics of mental and moral break-down among the very carefully selected troops of the American Army during their brief service in France and to the statistics (still very incomplete) of public assistance in the United States. The magnitude of the sums devoted to public and private charity is splendid evidence of the humanity of the American people; but a complacent acceptance of the state of affairs implied by it would show that their hearts are more excellent than their heads. The Monthly Bulletin of the Massachusetts Society for Mental Hygiene announces that "Last year [1922] there were 9,219 Joes who resided for varying periods in the county jails and houses of correction in Massachusetts." And Joe is the generic name by which the Bulletin designates men who come before the courts charged with criminal offenses which they commit by reason of their feeble-minded condition. If the same proportion holds good in the other States, it follows that in the year 1922 the jails and houses of correction of the whole country must have lodged some 300,000 such persons.

[1] "Social Evolution and Political Theory," New York, 1923.

tion, a selective death-rate is naturally and inevitably replaced by a selective birth-rate, they fail equally to see that some social control of this selective birth-rate is an indispensable condition of national welfare, a means which may be substituted for the operations of natural selection, enabling nations to secure the benefits of natural selection without inflicting its terrible cruelties. Hence they seek to disguise from themselves, by all manner of specious arguments, the importance of the native qualities of men, and to represent all possible changes of such qualities as of vanishingly small importance in comparison with the processes of social evolution.

This is the common method of avoiding in theory the difficulty of harmonizing evolution with ethics. And the desire to avoid or circumvent this difficulty is the unavowed ground of much of the common bias against recognition of native differences of value between individuals and races. But to take this line is merely to refuse to face the most fundamental and tremendous issue that confronts us. Civilization must not be content to avoid this issue, to shirk it, to be wilfully blind to it. The inevitable penalties of doing so are racial degeneration, cultural decay, and social chaos.

The truth is that the native differences between men, though they may seem small to a superficial view, are nevertheless vastly important.[1] It may be true that civilization may endure and even undergo further development, without any further evolution of the native qualities of men. But this can only be possible so long as the various peoples of the world continue to produce a fair proportion of individuals of the highest type, men and women capable of fully assimilating the culture transmitted to us by our forefathers and of further refining and improving it.[2]

[1] These differences, no doubt, are small in comparison with the total native endowment of the average human being. But to call them "small" in any other sense would be gravely misleading.

[2] Since the opinion of one who has made a life-long study of the mental qualities of men will hardly carry the same weight as that of a man who has devoted himself to the study of the physical peculiarities of race, I cite in support of my position the judicial statement of a leading anthropologist. Professor R. B. Dixon writes, in his recently published "Racial History of Man," as follows: "That there is a difference between the fundamental types in quality, in intellectual capacity, in moral fibre, in all that makes or has made any people great, I believe to be true, despite what advocates of the uniformity of man may say" (p. 518). Further, he writes, in reference to the present tendency to mingling of all races: "To make sure that from this newest, most tremendous fusion, the most perfect product shall result, can it be denied that we should seek

That is to say that, though much may yet be done to improve the civilization of the leading peoples of the world, so long as they suffer no deterioration of native quality, nevertheless we cannot rationally hope for further social progress nor even for the maintenance of social life at its present modest level, if our populations are destined to continued deterioration of quality. From which it follows that an ethical system that tends to such deterioration is at its best an imperfect, an incomplete, ethics. There, in brief, is the biological case against the universal systems, the case for the necessity of recognizing the validity of National Ethics, and the need for effecting a synthesis of the two systems.

---

to compound it mainly from the best? And not only from the best so far as race is concerned, but best in individual quality within the racial group, for that within the group there is difference in quality is obvious. In the past, when racial mixture was so often brought about through invasion or conquest, a certain rough selection was exercised in this respect. . . . To-day this more or less automatic process of selection exists but little, if at all . . . it seems doubtful if any man-made substitute can fully compensate for the kind of natural selection which for accounted ages has controlled in this respect the development of mankind."

To which I would add that the chief difficulty in the way of preventing the racial decay which is here hinted at by Prof. Dixon, as the probable fate of all mankind, is the difficulty of bringing the thoughtful part of the race, biased as it is by its acceptance of the Universal Ethics, to recognize the facts and admit the requirements of the present world-situation.

The great need of our time is, then, such a system, an ethico-political philosophy that will harmonize the principles of Universal and of National ethics. It must be a utilitarian philosophy, in the sense that it must formulate its precepts and pass its moral judgments with reference to an ethical goal that lies in the distant future. And it must give due recognition to two conditions, which are to be fostered and preserved as means for the attainment of the goal, namely: (1) nations as the bearers of culture and moral tradition; (2) the native qualities of the populations of each nation. Without the former means, namely, well-organized nations each maintaining and developing its national traditions, social life will fall into chaos, no matter how excellent the qualities of the peoples. Without the latter, namely populations that maintain their qualities undiminished from generation to generation, the nations cannot thrive and international harmony cannot be attained.

We may lay down a third essential principle of the required ethico-political system—namely, every man is to be regarded, not only as an end in himself, but also as an element in the life of the nation and, therefore, as a means to the supreme ethical goal; that is to say, his welfare must be in some degree subordinated to that of the nation. Yet the national organization must be such as favors the highest development of personality; for, without such development of individuals, the nation itself cannot thrive. Hence, the nation, though it may demand unlimited sacrifices from all its citizens, must secure as much freedom to every individual citizen as is consistent with its own welfare, must put only such limits to his freedom as its own needs imperatively require.

Political writers have often described the institution of representative democracy as a mere consequence of the fact that the large size of modern nations renders direct democratic procedure impossible. But that is, I think, a very serious error. Whether we consider American or British democracy, the historical truth would seem to be that the institution of representative democracy was governed, not merely by regard for the welfare of its component individuals, but largely by regard for the welfare of the nation as such; or in other words, that the principles of National Ethics worked strongly in the minds of those who chiefly shaped the political development of these two peoples.

It seems to be equally true that the subversion of representative democracy, which already has gone far, has been due mainly to the fact that, while the principles of Universal Ethics have been generally and explicitly accepted, the principles of National Ethics have remained implicit, unformulated, and unacknowledged: so that whatever demands have been made in the name of Universal Ethics have seemed to the mass of mankind to be ethical, moral, or right; while all demands made in accordance with the unacknowledged principles of National Ethics have seemed to be unethical, because in conflict with the principles of the acknowledged universal code. Under these conditions it was, I say, inevitable that representative democracy should be subverted by the drift to ultra-democracy.

This then is the first of the political precepts dictated by the new ethics, namely, that democracy must be of the representative type, not merely as a matter of expediency, but in virtue of the ethical principle that the nation itself is an indispensable means to the ethical goal.

Two corollaries follow from the acceptance of this precept.

(1) The duty of the representative is not merely to secure the largest possible distribution of good things to his constituents; but rather he is charged primarily with the higher duty of conserving the moral and material resources of the nation and of guarding and developing its institutions, for the sake of the future welfare of the nation as the indispensable means to the ethical goal.

(2) The duty of the citizen in choosing his representative is to elect the man best qualified to discharge these national duties, rather than the man who is a true sample of any particular class of citizens, a class whose special interests he understands and might promote as the delegate of that class.[1]

These conclusions may be concisely formulated in the statement that the government required

---

[1] This principle is incompatible with any extreme form of Guild Socialism, Syndicalism, or any other "ism" that would put political representation on an occupational basis. Or, more generally, it is incompatible with the doctrine that the welfare of the nation may be secured by the mere conflict of interests of the various classes of citizens; a doctrine which seems to be widely accepted, and which, if not often baldly stated, has received some support from political philosophers.

by the new ethics is government by aristocracy, an aristocracy representative of the best tendencies of the democracy and responsible to the whole people.

The second great political precept, the full recognition of which is demanded by the new ethics, is that Internationalism, rather than Cosmopolitanism, is the true or desirable world-order. Nations and the spirit of nationality are to be recognized, not as unfortunate legacies from the past, not as survivals from a darker age, to be tolerated only until we can bring about their abolition without immediate social chaos; but rather as most precious products and instruments of the process of human evolution. For each nation is the indispensable bearer of the sum of national traditions without which civilized life is impossible. And each nation is, or should become, a moral organism capable of taking its place as a member of a society of nations and of undergoing a process of further moral evolution. In that society each nation must increasingly recognize the rights of all nations and its own moral obligations and duties as a member of that society.

This is the point where the new ethics will

encounter the most obstinate resistance from
the cynical scepticism of the exponents of
Universal Ethics and of ultra-democracy. For
these, while pretending that every man may be
expected to show a sensitive regard for the
welfare of all his fellowmen, no matter how
remote from him in place, in customs, beliefs,
aspirations, and interests, scoff at the notion that
nations may learn to conduct themselves as
moral organisms in a society of nations.

In this they completely overlook two facts of
fundamental importance: first, that each man
attains to whatever morality he may display
in virtue only of his coming under the influence
of the moral tradition; second, that this moral
tradition, of which the nation is the bearer, is
the product of a long evolution to which the
efforts of many exceptional men have contributed.

The hope that nations may attain to a decent
level of international morality in their dealings
with one another is far better grounded than the
hope that, under a cosmopolitan order, men
would continue to achieve the modest level of
moral conduct which is now the average level
of civilized mankind.

Such hope of the establishment of an effective tradition of international morality, of moral self-restraint in the conduct of each nation towards other nations, is the one hope of the world.[1] *There is no other conceivable world-order under which we may rationally expect or hope for continued progress or, indeed, for anything but general relapse into barbarism and world-chaos.*

Here, then, is the second and more important ground on which the new ethics demands that nations shall repudiate ultra-democracy, in favor of a representative democracy in which the aristocratic principle is given due weight. If each nation had duties to itself alone, it might perhaps indulge in any form of experiment in political organization, taking the risks of disaster

[1] We hear much talk of "international law"; but it cannot be too clearly recognized that the so-called international law is nothing other, or more than, a tradition of international morality, at present but feeble and of little effect. But all moral tradition becomes effective only through a long process, involving the efforts and sacrifices of a multitude of men of the better sort. Therefore we should not allow the present disorder of the world to drive us to a cynical or pessimistic view of the future development of international morality. As Baron F. von Hügel writes: we have to recognize "the State as essentially moral, as (after all) the creation, however spontaneous and necessary, of human beings, who begin to be, and who remain, human only so long as they possess, in any and all of their functions and formations, some interior striving, conflict, groping, ideal, all of an ever incomplete kind, never more than partially practised, yet none the less truly moral" ("The German Soul" p. 203).

on its own shoulders, without grave offense against morality. But no nation can live to itself alone; the welfare of all is increasingly dependent upon the welfare and the stability and the morality of each. Each nation has therefore grave moral obligations to all the rest. And the primary and most fundamental of these obligations of each nation is that it shall strive to achieve within itself such political organization as will enable it to discharge effectively all its other international duties.[1]

Now a nation organized as an ultra-democracy cannot hope to discharge its international obligations. Inductively and deductively it is only too clear that an ultra-democracy cannot be expected to act in international relations as a moral agent. This truth might be demonstrated at great length. I will venture to adduce only one illustration of it.

The Great War was the result of the total repudiation by one nation of Universal Ethics,

[1] That the development of internationalism depends upon and presupposes sound and vigorous nationalism was clearly recognized by Theodore Roosevelt. Shortly before his death, he wrote: "let us build a genuine internationalism, that is, a genuine and generous regard for the rights of others, on the only healthy basis:—a sound and intense development of the broadest spirit of American nationalism."

in favor of exclusively National Ethics. When that nation, Germany, launched itself upon its supreme enterprize of world-domination, Great Britain delayed hardly a single day to throw all her resources into the struggle for the defense of civilization. America, on the other hand, required nearly three years to make the moral decision and to begin to throw her immense resources on the side of international morality; a delay which proved disastrous, and almost proved fatal, to Western civilization.

Why this great difference between the two nations in the promptitude and efficiency with which they discharged their international obligations? Many partial explanations of the difference have been suggested. But the fundamental and true explanation is, I submit, the fact that in Great Britain the political organism retained more of the truly representative and aristocratic principle, had not drifted so far down the slope towards ultra-democracy as had the United States.

Americans commonly allege, truly I suppose, that Woodrow Wilson was justified in making every effort to keep the country out of the war, for nearly three years, because the people was not ready to play its part. It is said that, if his government had declared war at an earlier date, it could not have carried the people with it.[1] And what influence was it that, in the end, led the people to undertake the discharge of their international obligation? There was no essential change of the situation. No new moral issue arose. The moral issue was the same in 1914 as in 1917. The result was achieved through an intensive campaign of popular education, conducted by the best elements of the population. Now I suggest that, if the American nation had been organized on the true principles of representative democracy, which give due weight to the best elements, to the most instructed, to the most capable, to those in whom the moral tradition is most fully embodied, those elements, having molded public sentiment and being in a position to determine the issue of national deliberation, would have been able to bring the united nation rapidly and effectively to the discharge of its international obligation; in consequence, the world would have been

[1] This however was not the opinion of W. H. Page, whose published letters strongly support the view that Mr. Wilson used, with great effect, the prestige of his great office to suppress the sounder judgment and the more generous impulses of the American people.

spared immense sufferings and immense losses of life and of morale; in place of these losses, the world would have gained by a signal enforcement of the principles of international morality; and those principles would have been established on a new and vastly higher plane of stability and world-wide influence. This, then, is one historical illustration of the truth that a nation which allows itself to drift into ultra-democracy does a grave injury to civilization, to all the higher interests of mankind. [1]

[1] Here I will venture to hold up the mirror that enables a people "to see itself as others see it." In the midst of the war, that great American, W. H. Page, wrote of the impression made abroad by the supineness of the American nation as follows: "They say that the American democracy, since Cleveland's day, has become a mere agglomeration of different races, without national unity, national aims, and without courage or moral qualities." (Life and Letters, Vol. II, p. 32.) And he wrote also: "The United States stands for democracy and free opinion as it stands for nothing else and as no other nation stands for it. Now, when democracy and free opinion are at stake as they have not before been, we take a 'neutral' stand—we throw away our very birthright. We talk of 'humanity' all we like: we have missed the largest chance that ever came to help the large cause that brought us into being as a nation. And the people, sitting on the comfortable seats of neutrality upon which the President has pushed them back, are grateful for peace, not having taken the trouble to think out what Peace has cost us and cost the world." (Op. cit., Vol. II, p. 173.) That is to say, the American nation, in spite of the wide diffusion of benevolence and "idealism" throughout the people, was unable, through lack of the necessary national organization, to make effective this great store of "idealism," until the world had suffered vast and irreparable injuries.

At the present moment a similar situation confronts the American

Nations, then, owe, not only to themselves, but
also to the world the duty of developing and maintaining a political organization such as the new
ethics demands, an organization based on representative institutions which shall synthesize
the democratic with the aristocratic principle.
If all the leading nations can attain to such

---

nation. It may fairly be said that all Americans of goodwill and
enlightenment are advocating some form of coöperation with the
nations that are striving to ensure peace and international justice.
Yet the issue hangs in the balance. It remains very doubtful whether
these numerous best elements can leaven the lump. In a recent
number of "Our World," the editor writes: "The fact that the last
five presidents, Republican and Democrat alike, have favored it
[international coöperation] will not insure success. President
Harding saw clearly that carrying out this policy of American co-
operation with the world, especially as it was related to the World
Court, would require a tremendous struggle . . . the 'irreconcila-
bles' have already shown that they will push their opposition with
fresh vigor and force. . . . The new political forces that have
appeared in the farming section of the country will continue in
hostility, unless they are enlightened. The same will be true of
labor, in the mass, despite the stand for world coöperation taken
by some of its leaders. This is no endeavor to paint a gloomy picture but an effort, instead, to point to facts and conditions as they
are. And it may be safely added, as they will continue to be, unless
the people are convinced that the World Court and all other questions of coöperation with other countries, are pressing American
questions that affect the welfare of every man, woman and child
in the United States." This statement, that America can be moved
to action only when the majority of the people believe that their
individual self-interests are affected, this statement amounts to an
assertion that the decline from representative democracy to ultra-
democracy has already been completed in the United States.
Whether the writer realizes the gravity of the charge he makes
against the American democracy is not apparent from this article.

organization, then we may rationally hope to see the principles of international morality firmly established and duly observed. When that world-order shall have been achieved, any formal League of Nations will be unnecessary, as unnecessary as is any formal undertaking to act justly and considerately among men of honor and developed moral cultivation.

But, so long as nations are not so organized, so long as they are ultra-democracies, then, when some international crisis arises, they will require long years of effort on the part of the better elements of the population, before each nation can be brought to see its duty and to act as a moral agent. In such a world a League of Nations is perhaps the best that can be hoped for, imperfect and uncertain as its influence must always be as a substitute for international morality. [1]

I now come to the essential constructive suggestion to which all that I have said so far is but preliminary.

[1] It may be argued that, as the development of individual morality was possibly only in virtue of the protection of individual rights afforded by domestic law with all the apparatus for its enforcement, so also international morality can develop, only if the rights of nations are protected in an analogous fashion. I add some further discussion of this topic in the appendix.

The question before us is—How shall a nation be organized? What political national organization will most effectively render the nation a means towards the supreme ethical goal—the enduring and highest happiness of the greatest number of mankind in the near and in the distant future?

The two great functions of the nation must equally be kept in view: (1) the internal function, namely, efficient legislation and administration, making for the maintenance of a strong, sensitive, and moral public opinion, and for the preservation and, if possible, the improvement of the innate qualities of the people: (2) the external function, the effective coöperation with other nations in maintaining the principles of international morality.

The first practical principle essential to the true democracy is that not all individuals are qualified to share fully in the rights and duties of citizenship. This is true of all democracies, but especially of our vast modern nations, and most of all of the American people, made up as it is of so many heterogeneous elements of very different levels of culture and tradition and of diverse racial origins. Instead of blindly, indiscriminatingly, asserting the principle of "one adult, one vote," we must deliberately assert the principle—one qualified citizen, one vote. The franchise, municipal, state, and federal, must be denied to those who are obviously unfit to exercise it.

How then shall the unfit be defined? Two categories of the unfit can be defined easily, namely, the mentally deficient and the convicted criminals. Our highly organized medical science and institutions can select the former. Our legal institutions can select the latter. It seems to me a simple and indisputable truth that the mentally defective should never be enfranchised and that the convicted criminal should be disfranchised.

A third category of persons unfit to enjoy the full rights, because unfit to discharge the duties, of citizenship are the illiterate. This proposition also seems little open to dispute in the case of the completely illiterate, those who cannot read at all. For the whole machinery of modern democracy can only be worked on the supposition that the electors of representatives are capable of reading intelligently. Without this capacity they cannot exert, under the

modern conditions, any intelligent choice or
judgment. But illiteracy or literacy is a matter
of degree; and there is room for differences of
opinion as to the degree of literacy which should
be held to qualify for full citizenship. I, for one,
should have no hesitation in drawing the line
fairly high. I would not accept as a qualification a mere capacity to enjoy reading the details
of the latest murder. But the actual level of
qualification that should be demanded is a
question of detail. The assertion of the principle
is the main thing. All modern States maintain
elaborate systems of state-education. Especially
in this country there exists a finely graded and
universal system of free state-education. There
you have in working the machinery for separating the illiterates from the literates. Let it be
established that only those individuals who
attain or pass a certain grade of the educational
system are qualified for full citizenship, and
that no others shall be enfranchised.[1]

Those then are the three chief categories of
persons obviously unfit for full citizenship. Let

[1] A recent estimate, based on the statistics of the Illiteracy Com-
mission of the National Education Association, puts the number of
adults in the United Stated who are "illiterates" or "near-illiterates"
at 20 millions. ("Time" Vol. II, No. 7.)

it be recognized that full citizenship is a privilege entailing responsibilities, a privilege which any person may attain and retain only by showing himself to be fitted to exercise its responsibilities.

If the literacy requirements were drawn at a reasonably high level, the effect of this differentiation of two classes of citizens, the full citizens and the unenfranchised citizens, would be to cut out from the political organism its least efficient part, a part which is apt to exert a degrading effect upon the whole, constituting as it does an inert mass of voting power that lends itself to, and invites, abuses of every kind.

Let us for convenience distinguish the two classes by the letters A and C; A is the class of full citizens, C the class of unenfranchised citizens. If the literacy standard were made approximately the same in all countries, the two classes would be found in very different proportions in the various nations and countries. I suppose that in this country the C class might comprize perhaps one-quarter to one-third of the adult population. In Italy it would be larger, and in Mexico or India much larger still, and might rise as high as four-fifths or even nine-tenths or more of the whole. But, even in those countries, or in China, the adoption of the principle would render possible the introduction of representative democracy in a workable form, under which the proportion of the A class might steadily grow by the spread of education.[1]

[1] As a corollary of the educational qualifications, I would make the State system of education free to all, but compulsory on none, trusting that the desire for the privileges of full citizenship would be a sufficient incentive to all, or almost all, who are fitted by natural endowment to profit from the educational opportunities offered freely by the State.

The necessity for the adoption of such a mitigated form of democracy in Mexico has been well stated by President Obregon in the following passage: "In those periods in which Mexico has enjoyed peace, this peace has been produced by the rule of the cultured section of the people and the subordination of the unlearned class to that rule. If the country is to be governed in accordance with the rule of universal suffrage, then the majority of the population, that is to say, the illiterate section of it, will have the control of the cultured class. In other words, that class which for its own benefit was subordinated under the Spanish regime, which in the United States is kept under guardianship, would rule in Mexico. If such should be the case, we must in candor confess that the Mexican people are not capable of self-government. This is mere common sense. The Indians and illiterate class of Mexico do not know in some cases even the Spanish language, do not know the political constitution, and the functions of the different branches of the administration. If their vote is to decide, then they will be the tools of wire pullers who may preach to them democracy or communism or any other word which will excite them and stir them into warlike action; or they will be the raw material for the government electoral machine. In both cases the sober honest citizen prefers to abandon the field to his opponents because he can see no possibility of overcoming that machinery, nor is he disposed to compete in machinations. There is no country in the world in which the most intelligent and capable class, in the long run, does not obtain in the government the preëminence it

The separation of the C class from the class of
full citizens should serve to raise the standard of
intelligence and responsibility in the electorate,
and, in so doing, greatly diminish the present evils

---

deserves, unless there is some external power, which interferes with
the inner forces of that country.

"But on the other hand, if the Mexican people are left to their own
resources and discretion they will prove their capacity for self-
government, just as they give daily proofs of their intelligence as
members of the professional classes, and of their ability and honesty
as business men. If they do not find it necessary to misrepresent the
facts, they may start again that work of civilizing the Indians which
they undertook in the epochs of greater prosperity for Mexico.
Let the educated class of Mexico assume before the world the responsibility for the culture of their own fellow-citizens. They will
show that they are trustworthy.

"I am not advocating an autocratic irresponsible government;
what I believe is a primary necessity for the life of Mexico is to restrict the exercise of political rights in Federal matters to those who
at least know how to read and write, who thus have an opportunity
to know what politics and justice and political economy may mean.
If we continue the rule of universal suffrage, we may have the opposite
effect of what you had in the South, where the majority of the whites
suppressed the vote of the colored people, and we may be forced
to suffer the well-known evils of the reconstruction period, with all
the political manœuvres of the carpet-baggers. In Mexico the enormous majority of the unlearned class discourages and overcomes the
vote of the literate. If you remember the history of the Indian
territory of the United States, and the reasons why you were compelled to withdraw the political franchise from the Indians there,
you may realize that the present situation in Mexico is a mere
duplication of conditions in that territory; and you may be compelled to admit that my suggestion is the only possible solution for
the Mexican problem." He therefore proposes "a literary test for
the exercise of the franchise." ("Are the Mexican People capable
of governing themselves?" Journal of International Relations,
Vol. XI, 1920.)

of democracy, rendering possible a return to the practical recognition of an elected and responsible aristocracy. But it should be further used in the service of a purpose no less, perhaps even more important, namely, the preservation and possibly the improvement of the native qualities of the full citizens. Consider now how this great end may be served by the institution of the two classes of citizens.

We have seen how, under present conditions, there obtains in all civilized nations a tendency to deterioration of the population, owing to the relative infertility of the better endowed, the inverse correlation of fertility with degrees of natural endowment. Under the present order of society, the rapidly multiplying lower strata are constantly infiltrating into, and substituting themselves for, the higher strata; so that the general tendency in each new generation must be a lowering of the average level of endowment throughout the whole population.

Now suppose that intermarriage between the A and the C classes were strictly prohibited. We should then have a system under which the A class would constantly be purified, namely, by shedding off into the C class, first, all those of its members who by criminal conduct showed themselves unworthy of the privileges and responsibilities of their class, and, secondly, all those who, though born of parents of the A class, failed to qualify for admission to it. At the same time, it would be constantly recruited by the admission of the best progeny of the C class.

We should thus have a system under which the A class would enjoy the advantage of a stringent selection, without the infliction of the cruelty and suffering that are inevitable consequences of Nature's harsh processes of natural selection. In this way we should solve, so far as the A class was concerned, the seeming opposition between the cosmic and the ethical processes, on which Huxley so eloquently insisted as an ultimate and irresolvable disharmony of human life.

But I suggest that this most important result might be better achieved than by prohibition of marriage between persons of the A and C classes; namely, in the following way. A third class, of status intermediate between A and C, should be legally instituted. This class, call it B, would have a probationary status. Every candidate for admission to the A class would have to spend at least twenty or twenty-five

years of his life as a probationer in the B class
before admission to A. But the children of
parents both of whom belonged to the A class
would have the status of the B class as their
birthright; and, on attaining adult life, they
would be, if otherwise qualified, admitted to the
A class. On the other hand, children born of
parents, either of whom was of the C class,
would have the status of the C class; if and when
they passed the qualifying educational test,
they would enter the B class as probationers;
and only after twenty years of this probationary
status, with due discharge of its recognized
obligations, would they be admissible to the A
class. This would be the recognition of the
sound principle that, not the individual, but the
family is the unit of society.

In addition it might be wise to enact, as a
discouragement of intermarriage between the
classes, that any citizen of the A class who
married a member of the C class should *ipso
facto* lose his A status and revert to the C class.

In this way the nation would achieve the
benefits of a simple caste-organization, namely,
the preservation of the qualities of the superior
strains, while avoiding those features which

condemn to stagnation every society founded upon a rigid caste-system, namely, the discouragement of ability and ambition and the prevention of character and capacity from rising in the social scale and exerting the influence that should be accorded to them. For the classes would not be hereditary castes.[1]

The establishment in all civilized nations of a three-class system, such as I have briefly sketched, would bring three great advantages.

First, it would secure that in each nation political power would rest in the hands of a reasonably select body of citizens, men and women who would be capable of understanding and of valuing and preserving the national traditions, who might be trusted to prefer

[1] Some of my readers may exclaim—"But the men of the C class would be mere serfs; and we cannot for a moment contemplate a return to serfdom for any part of our population." The answer is that men of the C class would not be serfs; they would be free men, free to sell their labor, to choose their place and mode of life, enjoying all the rights of citizens, except the right to vote and possibly also the right to unlimited and indiscriminate procreation. It may be pointed out also that the bulk of the colored people of the United States, both of Negro and Indian blood, have long been practically, and in part legally, restricted to the C status. My proposal therefore involves, so far as the United States are concerned, merely the cessation of racial discrimination and the explicit recognition and legal regulation of a state of affairs already existing in an unjust and disorderly fashion.

representative democracy to ultra-democracy
and to select, as their representatives, persons of
outstanding capacity and merit. Active participation in political life would thus be restored
to the position of high honor which is proper to
it; and the best men, no longer fearing utterly
ignorant and incapable electors, would be glad
to undertake these honorable tasks. Secondly,
each nation would be fortified against that most
fatal tendency which has played a great part in
destroying most of the civilizations of the past,
namely the tendency to die away at the top.
Thirdly, the class of full citizens would be protected against the lowering of its average quality
by the immixture of blood of inferior quality;
and so it might rationally hope to preserve itself
from deterioration and even slowly to improve
its quality from century to century.

One important problem remains to be lightly
touched. It is certain that the population of the
world cannot long continue to multiply itself
as it did in the great era that is now drawing to
a close, the era of rapid exploitation of the
world's reserves of energy and of consequent
rapid multiplication of men.

Continuance of such rapid multiplication

would render futile all hope of abolishing war
and of improving the lot of the mass of mankind.

The world must soon return in this respect
to the normal condition, that is to say, a condition of approximately stationary numbers. Since
we cannot permit the return of the more primitive agencies by means of which population has
been restricted in the long ages preceding the
industrial era, namely, abortion, infanticide,
epidemic and endemic disease, high infant mortality, and warfare, we must adopt the only
alternative, namely, deliberate regulation of its
population by each nation. Throughout the
development of our western civilization, such
control seems to have gradually supplanted in
large measure the primitive methods. Society
embodied in its customs and institutions the
view that marriage and the production of a
family are properly the privileges of those citizens who show themselves best fitted to assume
the responsibilities of those privileges. In the
towns and among the artisan classes, this result was in a large measure achieved by the institution of apprenticeship and craft-guilds; under
this system it was practically impossible for a man
to marry before he became a master craftsman

and a member of the guild. In the country the
same result seems to have been secured in large
measure by the fact that the common laborer had
to postpone marriage, until he could procure a
house and perhaps a farm of his own.[1]

[1] His position was, it would seem, very similar to that of the disappearing New England figure, the hired man of the farmer. On this topic see Mr. Carr Saunders' "Population Problem." He cites the conclusions of a Danish investigation by Rubin: "These obstacles to marriage in the case of the laboring class caused marriage to be postponed by men in this class. . . . Even though the social and economic structure of the community of old restrained one section of the population—the dependent section—from marriage, the other part of the population, the independent section, married far earlier than nowadays. . . . Those who could marry early, then, did so. But those who were unable to marry till late in life—when they no longer held the position of journeymen, labourer, etc.,—yet married. . . . In spite of the fact that in the independent section of the community marriage took place, as a rule, at an earlier age in the eighteenth century than it does now, the average age of marriage was yet higher at that time, because the more numerous dependent class married later. . . . The state of things indicated above is that typical of mediæval Europe and lasted up to the industrial revolution" (p. 265). Again he writes: "Far more important than any particular disabilities regarding marriage which attach to serfs are the conditions making very difficult any increase in population which are always found among cultivators. When a village has as many hands as it requires, the number of houses is not increased. Speaking generally of the Middle Ages, Pollard says that 'the number of holdings was almost stationary and the number of families fixed. The number of hands in a village found to be required would be about that which experience had shown to produce the largest average income. Any further increase is made very difficult, if not impossible. Country life was as elsewhere rigid in its habits; young people found it difficult to establish themselves till some married pair had passed from the scene and made a vacancy in their own parish; for migration to another parish was seldom thought of by an agricultural

At the present time all such social control has been abolished. The State and a multitude of

---

labourer. . . . Such always are the conditions among cultivators in a settled country; it is forced to the notice of everyone that not more than a certain number of hands are required and postponement of marriage is thus imposed upon the younger people. Neither land nor houses are available for them at an early age. Before the Reformation, not only were early marriages determinately discouraged, but the opportunity for them did not exist. A labourer living in a cottage by himself was a rare exception to the rule; and the work of the fields was performed generally . . . by servants who lived in the families of the squire or farmer, and who, while in that position, commonly remained single, and married only when by prudence they had saved a sufficient sum to enable them to enter some other position'" (p. 280). Of the towns, we read: "In essence the medieval town was the formation of guilds of merchants and craftsmen. . . . Membership of a guild was a birthright or an inheritance, and newcomers could only enter after a long period of apprenticeship. The result of this system of apprenticeship was to bring about the postponement of marriage, and thus to limit the undue increase of population. The position of a son who acquired a holding when his parent died is analogous to that of an apprentice who cannot set up as a master till given permission by the proper authorties. It is quite plain that in the eyes of the ordinary man in the sixteenth century one of the advantages of a system of compulsory apprenticeship was that it prevented youths marrying at a very early age. . . . Rubin . . . sums up the position in these words: 'The domestic servant class, then as now, was unmarried, but that class was much more numerous than at present. Subordinates in the industrial class and in handicrafts were not, as in our own time, free and independent, but lived for the most part in the houses of their masters, and, at any rate, were accustomed to wait until they became masters before marrying. . . . The same rule applied to other journeymen in various employments, whether in town or country.' Thus in the town as well as on the land the pressure was at work. The result was twofold. Marriage was made difficult, and many sought refuge in lifelong celibacy in religious institutions. Again, a standard of skill was insisted upon which tended to ensure that young husbands would be able to support a family, as well as ensuring that they

charitable agencies undertake to provide for every
child that any couple may fortuitously bring into

---

would not have a family at all until there was a place for them"
(p. 282). In addition various States enforced laws against the marriage of unqualified persons; *e.g.* in Wurtemberg no subject could
marry until he possessed "the right of a member of a community
or a settled non-freeman. But even such a one must prove to the
magistrate before his marriage that he possesses sufficient means of
subsistence. The want of such means of subsistence is considered
as existing, (a) in every one who is not primarily qualified in the
exercises of a liberal art or science, or for exercising on his own account, commerce, a profession, agriculture or some other business
sufficient for the independent support of a family; and (b) in every
one who, at the time of the intended marriage, is the subject of political or police investigation, for vagabondage, prodigality, habitual
idleness, notorious propensity to drinking, or repeated fraud, theft
or begging . . . or has received assistance from public funds for
his own support" (p. 283). I cite this evidence at some length
because it reveals the secret of the control of population in Europe
from the early medieval to the modern period. No doubt the older
more primitive checks remained operative in some degree, as they still
do; but in the main they seem to have been replaced by a system
of more or less deliberate social control.

And a point of extreme importance is that this social control
must have operated in the main eugenically, confining parenthood
to the prudent, the competent, the industrious, the skilful and the
successful. This social control, continued through several centuries
must have done much to maintain the qualities of the populations
by which it was exercised and may even have raised considerably
the average level of "civic worth." Two influences have combined to
suspend in the modern era this social control and to reverse the
eugenic tendency to breed from the upper strata of society; first, the
social chaos of the industrial age; secondly, the unchecked extension
of the universal ethics at the cost of national ethics, leading to a
state of affairs in which the privileges of marriage and parenthood
are regarded as the right of every man without respect to his personal qualifications for discharge of the correlative responsibilities.

In modern discussions of the minimum wage this all-important
aspect of the social problem is never considered; it is assumed with-

existence; and custom and the Universal Ethics approve early marriage for all and unlimited procreation among the lower strata of the populace.[1]

In the period upon which we are now entering, a return to severe restriction of reproduction is inevitable. All experience shows that, in the absence of social regulation and under the unmitigated sway of the Universal Ethics, this restriction will tend to be effected in the various social strata in direct proportion to their civic worth. In other words, each generation of the population will be in the main the progeny of the least competent, the least self-controlled, the least successful members of the preceding genera-

---

out question that every man has the right to be a parent and therefore to receive a wage sufficient for the support of a family. Yet even the modern reformer, swayed purely by Universal Ethics, does not venture to be consistent; for consistency would lead him to demand for every man a wage capable of supporting in comfort a family of some fifteen children.

In the small State of Massachusetts an alarming proportion of the State's revenue is expended upon public assistance, and in addition there are, I am told, as many as 140 distinct charitable associations which devote all their resources to bringing up the children of those who are incompetent to discharge the responsibilities of parenthood.

[1] It is sometimes asked—Why does the agricultural population of Denmark prosper exceedingly, while that of England is chronically in difficulties? And no answer is found. May it not be that the answer is to be found in the fact that the industrial revolution has maintained conditions of deterioration in the agricultural class in England for more than a century; while in Denmark something of the medieval system has been maintained with consequent preservation of native qualities?

tion; society will continually renew itself from the bottom and will continually die away at the top. This disastrous tendency can only be counteracted by a deliberate social control dictated by the principles of National Ethics, the ethics which recognizes the nation, as an essential means towards our ethical goal, and demands that the rights of the individual be subordinated to, and in some degree determined by, the needs of the nation.

Some such social organization as I have suggested would enable this most necessary social control of reproduction to be effected in a manner conducive to national prosperity and the advance of civilization. For it is obvious that a wise social regulation would aim at, and would know how to secure through the agency of custom, of social institutions and, if necessary, of legislation, a restriction of reproduction among the citizens of the unenfranchised class, a restriction as severe as the circumstances of the time might demand.[1]

[1] As an ultimate consequence of such social organization, we might look forward to a time when the whole population of the world would consist of the A class alone, the B and C classes having dwindled to the point of extinction. Then, and not before, our descendants might hope to see throughout the world the successful working of pure democracy, according to the formula "one adult, one vote."

If such restriction were effectively maintained, the class of full citizens might be trusted to regulate for themselves their reproduction-rate; and this class, relieved both of the economic competition of an excess of population swarming up from below, and from the evil influence of that excess of wealth and luxury which the more successful classes now obtain, through the exploitation of the labor of these masses of low-level population, the class of full citizens, I say, might under these conditions be expected to exercise in due measure the privileges of marriage and of parenthood. For, under the influence of an ethics in which the national principle was duly recognized, the function of parenthood would be restored to the position of honor that it has enjoyed in every healthy and stable society. We might hope to see the family reëstablished as the foundation of the State, as the true social unit, and as the nursery of those national traditions which alone raise us above the level of savage life and by the development of which alone mankind may hope to rise to higher and ever higher levels of happiness and culture.

APPENDIX

Outline of the One and Only Practicable Plan for Bringing About the Disarmament of Nations and the Reign of International Justice

In these supplementary pages I desire to make certain suggestions towards solving the problems of international relations. While sympathizing strongly with those who have instituted the League of Nations and who hope to see it increase steadily in authority and efficiency, I yet recognize the great force of the considerations that have hitherto prevented the American people from entering it.

Any nation that enters the League commits itself to the sacrifice of its sovereign rights in an undefined and unlimited degree.[1] In consequence

[1] The American objection to adhesion to the League has rested mainly on the ground that Article 10 of the Covenant of the League commits each member nation to the obligation of taking up arms in the defense of other nations unjustly attacked. This is a very grave commitment of indefinite range and magnitude. The advocates of

215

it remains only too probable that situations may arise (as in the case of Italy at the present moment—September, 1923) under which a member of the League will regret its adhesion and will threaten to break away from it, perhaps at the cost of destroying the League. It seems, therefore, that the instituting of the League was too large a change to be made at a single step. I agree with many other publicists in holding that it would have been wiser to institute at the present time a permament court of international justice. Such a World Court would interpret and enforce the terms of existing treaties; and it might be hoped that the Great Powers would enter into a series of treaties (such as the Washington Disarmament Treaty) looking towards the enforcement of peace and international jus-

American coöperation in the League attempt to exhibit it as of secondary importance. Thus Justice J. H. Clarke, one of the most generous of these advocates, said (in his address on behalf of the League of Nations Non-Partizan Association): "But, even this remote possibility of war within the League can come to us under Article 10 only with the consent of our own representative on the Council, for such a decision under it must be a unanimous one, and with the consent also of our Congress, for it is too clear for discussion that the treaty-making power is subject to the constitutional limitation that only Congress can declare war, and this all the other nations know as well as we and they are dealing with us on this understanding." It is clear that if the United States, and if other States, give to the League only such qualified adhesion as is here implied, its power to enforce its decisions must remain very limited.

tice. The terms of such treaties, signed by the various Great Powers, would then assume the status of international law, law binding upon all nations and enforced by the rulings of the World Court. In this way we should advance from the present position, in which no international law (*loi*) exists, but only partially recognized principles of international right (*droit*), to one in which all nations would be bound and forced to obey certain explicitly defined and limited principles of international law (law in the full sense of the word, only if the World Court wielded the power to enforce its rulings). [1]

Perhaps the most important of all such international laws would be one forbidding any nation to proceed to military action without having first stated its case to the world and having allowed a certain space of time to elapse between such statement and its first attempt to apply armed force to the remedy of its complaint.

A World Court, proceeding on these lines, might prove to be a sufficient protection of the rights of nations and a sufficient gaurantee

[1] For, by 'law in the full sense of the word,' I mean law that can be enforced, or law supported by effective sanctions, sanctions which, if they fail to secure observance of the law, will secure adequate punishment of infringement.

against unprovoked or unjustifiable attacks by one nation upon another (prcvided always the Court had the power to enforce its rulings). Under its protection the smaller nations, and perhaps even the Great Powers, might become content to live without military establishments.

If such a World Court, after some experience of its working, were found inadequate to the needs of the world, its existence and operation would have paved the way for the further and more extreme step of instituting a League of Nations with powers of international legislation, a parliament of all mankind.

Whatever form of International Authority is to become the safeguard of nations, whether a League of Nations, a World Court, or some other institution not yet foreshadowed, two great obstacles to its establishment, permanency, and efficiency remain to be overcome. These two obstacles are already very obvious to the world. I will state each one very concisely, and then put forward two suggestions which, I venture to think, are perfectly practicable and capable of overcoming these two obstacles respectively.

The less serious of these two difficulties is that

of determining justly and acceptably the extent to which each nation shall be represented in the constitution of the International Authority. It cannot reasonably be expected that the Great Powers would long be content with an International Authority in which each of the smaller nations should be represented as strongly as any Great Power. In such a body, any Great Power, or even any combination of Great Powers, would be liable to find itself out-voted and overruled by a combination of such States as Liberia and Haiti, Siam, Thibet, Afghanistan and Ethiopia.

If such a state of affairs should arise in relation to some vital interest of the Great Powers, the International Authority would be destroyed by the tension within it: it would explode, and all the work of international organization would have to be taken up anew on wiser lines.

Can we, then, adopt for the International Authority the principle of representation of Nations or States in proportion to the numbers of their populations? That also is an obviously impracticable plan. The Great Powers will not be content to be completely outweighed by India or China; nor would the secondary European nations readily accord to Java or to Siam an influence greater than their own.

This difficulty would no doubt be less serious in the institution of a World Court than in the organization of a League of Nations. For, since the sphere of authority of the World Court would be clearly defined and limited, nations would engage themselves to the acceptance of all its findings more readily than they would bind themselves to observe every law that might be promulgated by a League of Nations; and they would feel less strongly the need for adequate representation in the personnel of the Court than in that of the League.

Nevertheless, even the judicial deliberations of the Court would be liable to be influenced to an incalculable extent by the national sentiments of its members, no matter how honestly they might strive to maintain a strict impartiality.

I suggest that this difficulty may best be met in the following way. Let each nation be represented in the International Authority (whether Court or League) to an extent proportional to its annual budget. Or, since it would not be possible to secure any very strict proportion, the nations might be grouped for this purpose in some five or more classes, according to the magnitude of the average annual budget or revenue of each one.

The justification for this arrangement is the fact that the annual expenditure of a nation corresponds roughly to the extent of its power, and to the magnitude of its interests in the economic world-order. It would thus be an approximately just arrangement and one which all nations might be expected to accept. Further, it would be one which would secure automatic readjustment of the representations of the various nations, as in the course of time their relative status as World-powers might undergo more or less rapid changes. Thus, if any nation, such as Siam or Mexico, were to repeat the recent history of Japan and to spring almost suddenly into the rank of a Great Power, its representation in the International Authority would undergo automatically and without friction a corresponding increase.

An objection to this arrangement of some weight is the fact that those States in which the nationalization of industries and services was more general than in others would secure unduly large representation. And this fact might constitute an undesirable inducement to increasing nationalization. Also, it may, perhaps, be argued that it would unduly favor those nations which expended large sums on military equipment and training. I suggest, therefore, as an alternative form of the same principle, that the representation of each nation in the International Authority might be made proportional, not to its total annual expenditure, but to that part of the revenues of the State devoted to public education. Such expenditure may, I think, be fairly regarded as the best measure of the extent to which any nation may justly claim to make its voice heard in all international deliberations and decisions. And, if this arrangement should stimulate any nation to increase the amount of its expenditure upon education, that result would be of benefit both to itself and to the whole world.

The second and greater obstacle in the way of the institution and effective operation of any International Authority is the difficulty of securing to it the power to enforce its rulings. This problem is of the first importance in relation to the preservation of peace and the disarmament of nations.

There are, I think, but few nations which would not be glad to rid themselves of the burden of armaments, if they knew that in all international questions they had the right to submit their case to a World Court, and if they were absolutely assured that this World Court had the power to secure to them this right and to enforce its own rulings.   But, so long as there can be any doubt, any suspicion, concerning the absolute supremacy of the physical force wielded by the Court or of the effectiveness of its control over its means of enforcement (its power to put such force immediately into action with overwhelming effect against any nation, no matter how powerful, or any combination of two or three strong nations) so long will nations be unwilling to disarm themselves completely and to entrust their defense entirely to the principles of justice and to the strong arm of the International Authority.

There are idealists who will say that the International Authority needs no armed forces, that its moral authority should and must suffice.   I will not waste words in demonstrating the unpractical nature of this contention.   We are concerned with the world as it is and may be, not

with the world as we should like to have made it.
If men and nations had attained to such a level
of morality that the International Authority required no powers of compulsion, the world would
already have passed beyond the need for any
such Court or League.

Three proposals, and, I believe, three only,
have hitherto been made for meeting this difficulty.

First, it has been proposed that the International Authority should rely upon the weapon
of economic pressure or boycott; that, if any
nation should refuse to abide by its ruling, it
should forbid all other nations to trade with it.

This, no doubt, would be a powerful weapon.
But would it have that quality of absolute and
immediate efficiency which is indispensable, if
the complete confidence and sole trust of all nations is to be placed in the protective power of
the International Authority? I think not. It
would have two great defects. On the one hand,
the weapon of economic boycott would be slow
in operation, and slower in proportion to the
power and resources of the recalcitrant nation to
which it might be applied. Imagine that Germany had established economic and military

dominance over Russia. Might she not venture to defy the threat of economic boycott? And, if the boycott were applied, might she not overrun and destroy one or more of her neighbours before the economic pressure could reduce her to submission?

On the other hand, it would be difficult or impossible to enforce the observance of the boycott on all other nations. In the circumstances just now imagined, it might well be that the smaller neighbours of the recalcitrant Great Power would be tempted to throw in their lot with hers. We might then see the tragi-comedy of one half the world boycotting the other half, to the detriment of all nations, to the frustration of the International Authority, and perhaps to its disruption.

A second plan proposed is that the International Authority should have the right to call upon each and all nations to furnish contingents towards the formation of an international army and navy, which force would then execute its behests. This also would involve a slow and cumbrous procedure; and it would provide no absolute guarantee of success, even in the long run, if it were put into operation.

A more serious objection to this plan is the fact that it might prove impossible to put it into operation. In these days of democratic government, it might well happen that one or more of the nations called upon to furnish contingents (and in certain eventualities the contingents might need to be very large) would find itself unwilling or unable to respond. The mass of the population might threaten a general strike or otherwise effectively prevent even a well-intentioned government from living up to its obligations.[1]

Further, this plan, apart from the slowness and uncertainty of the procedure proposed, would have the drawback that it would involve each nation in the obligation to maintain armed forces of considerable magnitude. And, in so far, it would constitute a constant threat to peace and an absolute bar to general disarmament.

[1] Something of this sort did actually occur in Great Britain, when it was proposed to send a contingent to aid in the defense of Poland against the aggression of Soviet Russia. It is obvious also that, if States are to give only such qualified adhesion to the League as is proposed for the United States by Justice Clarke (compare footnote on page 215), *i.e.* armed support, when requested, only if and when the national parliament shall have approved such support, the protection offered by the League of Nations to any nation, threatened or attacked, must be lacking in two essentials, namely, first, rapidity of application, secondly, guarantee of adequacy when applied.

The third plan proposed is that the International Authority should maintain its own armed forces for constant readiness to enforce its rulings. This plan, if adopted on a sufficiently large scale, might seem to afford better assurance of rapid and effective action in support of international law. But against it also would lie certain very grave objections. In order to provide sure protection to unarmed nations, the army and navy to be maintained by the International Authority would require to be very large. An army of less than a million men, highly trained and equipped, would be *pour rire;* and the navy would have to be proportionally large. The expense of maintaining these large forces would be very great. But, apart from that, the maintenance under arms of a very large mercenary army of professional soldiers (and a corresponding navy) would be in itself a very grave evil and even a positive danger to the world. Empires have been overthrown by such armies in the past. It would not be possible to guarantee to the International Authority its control over such an army. Even if there were no risk that such an army as a whole might get out of hand at any time, there would remain another great risk. Such an army would necessarily be composed of men of many nationalities; and the men of any one nationality would necessarily be grouped in units, such as divisions or army corps. This being so, there would always be the danger that one part of the army might refuse its coöperation or might even take up arms against another part.

It may be suggested that the objections I have raised to both the second and third plans would be very much diminished, if under the third plan all nations would consent to complete disarmament, or if, under the second plan, each nation would consent and faithfully agree to maintain only such armed forces as might be permitted and enjoined upon it by the International Authority, holding the whole of such forces at the disposal of that authority. It is true that, if either arrangement were practicable, the efficiency of the corresponding plan would be greatly increased. But neither arrangement is practicable. Nations are willing neither to abolish nor seriously to limit their armaments, *unless their protection can first be absolutely guaranteed.* Further, even if all nations consented to such limitations, it would not be possible for the International Authority to ensure the exact observance of those limits; and, even if it were able to do this, it would not be possible to prevent doubt and suspicion and anxiety from growing up on all sides. To make in secret very considerable preparations for war would be so easy for any nation that universal confidence in the universal observance of the prescribed limitations could not be continuously maintained.

What then is to be done? Must we sorrowfully admit that the problem is beyond the possibility of all solution, that each nation must continue to arm itself to the teeth and to rely for its safety upon its own power of armed resistance and upon a shifting system of warbreeding alliances?

The foregoing discussion has made it clear that, if the International Authority is to assure to the Nations absolutely effective protection, if it is to confer on mankind the inestimable blessings of perpetual peace and universal disarmament, it must be furnished with a weapon of tremendous power, a weapon which can be maintained at small expense in perfect readiness for almost instantaneous action in any part of the world, a weapon that can be wielded by a small body of trained experts in a way that can overcome the resistance of an armed nation, a weapon which no nation can develop and perfect in secret.

If such a marvelous weapon can be found, our problem will be solved, the crux of the difficulty may be overcome, and the world may breathe freely once more.

It so happens that science has recently placed in our hands a weapon answering perfectly to all these essential requirements. It only remains for the Nations to place in the exclusive control of the International Authority this supreme weapon, this flaming sword of the Archangel of Peace. That Authority will need but to let its gleam be seen afar off, to make audible the sound of its swift annihilating rush through the skies, and the proudest nation, the greatest army, the most formidable navy, will lay down its arms, and Reason and Justice will prevail in all the earth.

The weapon I speak of is an efficient and exclusive air-force, equipped with all those terrific annihilating agencies the contemplation of which, as agencies of warfare, is even now holding the world in shuddering horror. Here is by far the greatest aggressive agency yet invented, or likely to be invented; and it will prove to be the greatest curse of the world or the greatest blessing that science has brought to mankind, according as we use it ill or well, as we turn it to bad or good ends.

I suggest, then, that the leading nations of the world authorize and instruct the International Authority to equip and maintain a small but highly efficient air-force, and that the prime article of International Law (to be established in the way suggested above, *i. e.*, by treaty between the Great Powers) shall be that no nation shall maintain an air-force of its own. And, in order to make this weapon of International Justice absolutely effective, it will be necessary to forbid absolutely (by similar process of International Law) all commercial and all other forms of aërial navigation. *The right to navigate the air must be confined absolutely to the air-force of the International Authority.* This drastic suppression of all other flying is both necessary and practicable.

It is necessary because, in the absence of such a ban, various nations would soon develop large fleets of commercial airships or airplanes; it would remain impossible to provide against the rapid conversion of them into instruments of aggression; therefore, confidence in the powers of protection of the International Authority, the prime condition of general disarmament and therefore of peace, could not be secured.

It would be practicable, because, unlike naval and military preparations, the training of an air-force cannot be carried on in secret. A principal feature of the training of the one sole and international air-force would be the patrolling of the whole earth, in order to observe and report any indications of unauthorized aërial activity. And there can be little doubt that such patrol could effectively secure this object.

This concentration of the control of all aërial navigation, and of all means of assault from the air, in the hand of the International Authority would, then, secure to it the means of immediate enforcement of its rulings. It would provide that completely effective sanction to International Law which is absolutely necessary, if the institution of any International Authority is to succeed in attaining its prime object, namely, the protection of Nations against unjust aggression and against the denial of their indisputable rights. Under the protection of an International Authority, thus effectively armed, armed with a thunderbolt of overwhelming power that could be launched against any State with a delay of only a few hours or days, every nation, it might fairly be hoped, would be willing and glad to divest itself of the burden of armaments. And, even if some Nations should continue to maintain armies and navies of great size, such forces would cease to be a cause of anxiety to the unarmed Nations.

The realization of this plan would bring to the world a further immense benefit. Namely, it would relieve all the world from that terrible threat under which the peoples of Europe are even now, in spite of the League of Nations, suffering acutely, the threat of attack from the air, coming perhaps suddenly, without a moment's warning, to devastate their cities and to spread disaster, mutilation, and death, on a scale hitherto only known in the convulsions of Nature.

It is difficult for Americans, or any others who were not under bombardment from the air during the Great War, to realize imaginatively the full horror of this threat. It is necessary to reflect on the following facts. France has already developed a very powerful air-force. Great Britain has felt herself compelled, in spite of great reluctance and her economic embarrassments, to renew her air-force and to vote £20,000,000 for this purpose. But more serious still is the fact that Soviet Russia is preparing an immense air-force. In a recent article,[1] Lt. Com. C. A. Tinker has described these Russian preparaions. He asserts that this action of the Soviet government is finding enthusiastic support in the press and among the populace. "While it is known that 300 airplanes built in Italy were bought by the Soviet Government last spring, the real power behind this movement is Germany. German manufacturers and operators have established plants and air lines in Russia, and German war pilots make up the flying personnel. This is a direct consequence of the scheme of the Allies to control German aviation since the war. By curtailing activity within German borders, the Allies have forced the Germans into other countries. German manufacturers are now engaged in producing airplanes

[1] *Christian Science Monitor*, Aug. 24, 1923. The same newspaper publishes a recent pronouncement of Premier Mussolini to the effect that Italy must have an air-force stronger than that of any other nation.

in Holland, Switzerland, Spain, Italy and Russia. Their enterprises in Russia, however, are on such a scale as to overshadow their efforts elsewhere. . . . The Junkers' Airplane Company of Germany has arranged for the creation of the Soviet Airfleet and it has built a huge plant on Russian territory for the purpose. A schedule of contracts calls for delivery, on or before April 1, 1924, of 3000 airplanes of every sort required for a complete military air-force— these are of the all-metal type—the last word in airplane construction. . . . This is enough to cause the French and British considerable worry as to what Russia means. To go further, the bugaboo of a German-Russian-Turkish alliance does not seem to down. Only recently Clemenceau called attention to the fact that behind Russia and Germany is the menace of Turkey, which, largely backed by Bolshevistic resources, becomes an enormous power for damage to western civilization."

The prospect raised by these facts is appalling. *No plan other than the one here proposed can relieve the world of this horrible nightmare.* No limitation of armies, navies, and air-fleets by general international agreement; no international army, navy, or air-fleet, nor all three combined, could make the Nations secure, and, still less, enable them to feel themselves to be perfectly secured, against this swift terrible incalculable menace. The desired security, the security which alone can induce Nations to disarm, and to regard military preparation as a thing of the past, can be attained only by the absolute prohibition of all aërial navigation to the nationals of all countries, except to the small body of aërial experts employed by the International Authority to carry out its orders. And only by maintaining such a body of aërial experts can the International Authority prevent the development of secret air-forces.

Two objections, and, I think, two only, can be raised against this plan.

First, it may be said, the air-force of the International Authority might mutiny and hold the whole world to ransom; as some years ago the crews of two Brazilian warships mutinied effectively against their government. This is not a real danger, for, though the personnel of the air-force would have the power to use a threat or even to do incalculable damage, all motive for such action would be lacking; a few men, professional experts carefully selected from all countries, would not be tempted to make themselves universally execrated by betraying the trust placed in them by the whole world, as the instruments of International Law.

The second objection has more weight. It will be urged that the proposed plan involves the suppression of a new agency of transportation vastly more rapid than any other conceivable, and that the giving up of this agency would be too great a deprivation to ask of the world.

In reply, it may fairly be asked whether any material deprivation could be too great, in proportion to the world-wide benefit to be brought by it, a benefit which will be felt by every human being and which will secure civilization against the menace now hanging over it like a dark thunder-cloud, the menace of self-destruction. And is it clear that aërial transportation is capable of conferring great benefits on mankind? Actual communication, in these days of telegraphy and radiograms, will not be facilitated by it. Only the transport of persons and of the less bulky kinds of merchandise, such as newspapers, will be accelerated. It is, to my mind at least, an open question, whether, apart from all military use of aërial navigation, the drawbacks attending the development of aërial transportation would not outweigh its benefits. Is it not a doubtful blessing that a man should be able to halve the time required for travel from London to Paris or New York? Is not the world already beginning to suffer from the tendency of men to flit rapidly from place to place in an almost aimless meaningless fashion? Is it certain that the descent upon France of multiplied swarms of foreign tourists would increase the affection of the French for America or for England? Would not a further great increase of facility of human transport take away one of the few remaining forms of romance? Would it not also tend to the spread of that vicious cosmopolitanism which consists in detachment from the traditions of one's own country? Under the head of "A 'Triumph' for Journalism" a newspaper[1] recently commented as follows on the first consignment of trans-continental mail by air from San Francisco to New York: "The flight which marked the culmination of long, patient and costly effort on the part of the Post Office Department, and in which

[1] *Christian Science Monitor*, Aug. 24, 1923.

were employed airplanes representing the final achievement of inventive effort, occupied thirty-eight hours. *The World* exultantly prints a fac-simile of the first page of a San Francisco paper which the inventive genius and the daring of men, aided by the resources of the Nation, had thus carried across the continent in less than two days. And what is the message conveyed to the world by this fortunate San Francisco news-paper? Across its first page, in letters of deepest black, appears the heading, 'Bandits Kill Poker Player!' Other large headings are: 'Posses Scour Mountain for Wounded Man'; 'Musical Comedy Stars Revealed as Agents in New York Bucket Shop Quizz'; 'Mrs. Kerr Fined $10 for Battery of Woman While Whipping Spouse.' The only other considerable head has to do with the enterprise of the Government in arranging the coast-to-coast flight by which all this impor-tant intelligence could be speeded across to the eager people of the Atlantic seaboard." And all this "important intelligence" might have come far more rapidly and cheaply by telegram.

I will add to this comment only one further consideration. When travel by airplane shall have become easy, cheap, and generally practised, the exploits of the motor-bandits of the present age will be thrown into the shade by those of the airplane-bandits of that rapidly approaching time. What police-force, what frontier-guards, will know how effectively to control these bandits and bootleggers of the air?

In view of these and of many similar considerations, I submit that the deprivation to be asked of the Nations, in resigning to the International Authority the exclusive right to make use of aërial navigation, would, in comparison with the benefits to be secured to all the world by such deprivation, be vanishingly small; and that, therefore, there is no serious objection to be raised against the plan here proposed.

It only remains to suggest how the International Authority is to be given this absolute and exclusive control over aërial navigation and the single air-force of the future. It may be hoped that, on ventilation of this plan, its advantages may appear so great and obvious that it will be accepted by all the Nations without exception. But this cannot be confidently predicted. I would urge, then, that its institution requires only the agreement of a group of Great Powers, with the adhesion of many of the smaller nations, an adhesion which many of them would give with enthusiasm. If any nation or nations, great or small, Great Britain, or Russia, or Germany, or France, or Guatemala, or Liberia, should refuse to consent to dispense with all aërial navigation, it, or they, should be told that great emergencies and world-wide dangers demand drastic remedies; that the world is now one, and that, just as no nation could be allowed to spread a deadly epidemic over the earth, so no nation can be allowed to endanger the peace of the world, to hold a terrible threat over the heads of all other nations, and to frustrate the world-wide desire for peace, disarmament, and the universal sway of International Justice; that, therefore, it is formally required by the agreed nations that it (or they) subscribe to the compact and faithfully observe its terms.

Lastly, I suggest that the United States Government should take the first step towards the realization of the plan here proposed, by issuing to all the Great Powers a formal invitation to coöperate in its institution and maintenance.

It will be observed that the plan would avoid the great objection raised against the present League of Nations (and especially against

Article X of the Covenant of the League); for it would not commit the United States, or any other State, to participation in European, or any other, war. Nor would it aim absolutely to prevent all war. Nations which might find a fair cause of quarrel would be at liberty to settle it by open warfare (exclusive of aërial warfare) so long as they abstained from the infringement of explicitly defined precepts of International Law.

It is noteworthy that, although the people of America have been hitherto spared the horrors of bombardment from the air, there is already on foot in the United States a strong movement for the limitation of national air-forces.[1] The Ameri-

---

[1] This movement should be strengthened by the following citation from the *Literary Digest:* "Military critics agree that there is no defense against this slaughter (from the air) at the present time, since, to put it professionally, the development of the airplane has put the offense far ahead of the defense in modern warfare. They agree also that, in case of another great war, so much of civilization would be destroyed that a return to something resembling the 'Dark Ages' would not be improbable. European civilization might easily be blotted out, agree the German and French authorities, and the British commentator, Commander Burney of the Navy, inventor of the paraplane during the war, and at present a member of Parliament, says that America would be anything but immune. He writes: 'There is scarcely a city in America which could not be destroyed, together with every living person therein, within, say, three days of the declaration of war [or perhaps three days before] between America and such a country as Japan on the Asiatic side, or a new group, such as Russia, Germany, and Bulgaria, from the European side. I do not say that this is possible to-day, but assuming that the techni-

can Legion is taking the lead in this movement
and gaining wide support. The Legion is re-
ported in the press to have issued recently a
proposal for an international air disarmament
conference and to have received favorable re-
plies from many influential persons, including
"22 United States senators, 93 representatives,
15 Governors, 216 newspaper editors, 44 college presidents and 82 other prominent citizens."
It is clear, therefore, that there is a large body
of influential opinion well prepared to regard
with favor the plan here proposed for the international use of air-force to suppress the use of
national air-forces and to secure the blessings of
disarmament and peace throughout the world.

ADDENDUM

It should be laid down as a preliminary principle that the persons who should draft the
clauses of the proposed international agreements
would be held personally responsible for the clear

cal possibilities which now exist in plan and on paper are translated
into actual fact within, say, ten years, I believe that I have not over-
stated the possibilities. . . . An airship leaving Japan could, within
forty-eight hours, be destroying San Francisco. Similarly an airship leaving Europe could be attacking New York in less than forty
hours from the time of her departure.' "

and unambiguous phrasing of each and every clause. If any such persons were to be found guilty of having drafted clauses in the ambiguous style of the notorious clause of the Armistice of 1918 governing reparations, of the clause of the Panama Canal Treaty stipulating for equality of treatment, or of the equally notorious and ambiguous clause of the Treaty of Versailles stipulating the right of the Allies to take steps for the enforcement of payment of reparation in case of default by Germany; in any such case, the persons found guilty should be hanged, drawn, and quartered, and their heads should be set up on pikes before the Lincoln Memorial in Washington, D. C.

NOTE ON THE BOK PEACE PLAN

THE announcement of the award of the Bok Peace Prize and the publication of the selected plan,[1] while this book is in the press, lead me to make the following comments reënforcing the argument in favor of the plan sketched in the foregoing appendix.

The essence of the Bok Peace Plan is the suggestion that the United States shall enter the Permanent Court of International Justice and shall coöperate with the League of Nations without full membership at present. The plan proposes also that Articles X and XVI of the Covenant of the League of Nations be either dropped altogether or so amended and changed as to eliminate any suggestion of a general agreement to use coercion for obtaining conformity to the pledges of the Covenant.

[1] Chosen by a jury of eminent persons as "The best practicable plan by which the United States may coöperate with other nations to achieve and preserve the peace of the world."

The Plan might well provoke me to many comments, but I desire only to comment upon it in so far as it affords further ground for urging my own plan, not as a rival or alternative, but as a necessary supplement.

First, I would point out that the Bok Plan, if it were accepted by the United States in its present form, would inevitably suggest to the other nations that the United States desires to reap the benefits of coöperation with the League of Nations without sharing in the responsibilities, the burdens, and the sacrifices which full membership in any effective League must impose on all its member-nations and more especially upon the more powerful of them. This would be an unfortunate impression from every point of view. It might lead other nations to regard somewhat cynically that American "idealism" of which they have heard so much and so often.

Secondly, the fact that the jury, eminent persons known to represent all that part of the American public which favors International Coöperation, has chosen this plan, out of some 22,000 plans submitted to it, shows very clearly that even the most internationally minded and idealistic part of the American people entertains no hope that the United States can be induced to commit itself to participation in either the use ᵻf national forces or the application of inter-national boycott for the protection of unoffend-ing nations against unjust aggression. For the obligations of this kind laid upon its members by the existing League of Nations (defined in Articles X and XVI of the Covenant) are of a vague ill-defined nature; they are very far from being of such clearly defined and binding a na-ture as would ensure effective coöperation from all or any of its members. ᵻ   Yet the Bok Peace

---

ᵻ Article X runs: "The Members of the League undertake to re-spect and preserve as against external aggression the territorial integ-rity and existing political independence of all Members of the League. In case of any such aggression or in case of any threat or danger of such aggression the Council shall advise upon the means by which this obligation shall be fulfilled."   And Article XVI, as amended, reads: "Should any Member of the League resort to war in disregard of its covenants under Article 12, 13, or 15, it shall *ipso facto* be deemed to have committed an act of war against all other Members of the League, which hereby undertake immediately to subject it to the severance of all trade or financial relations, the prohibition of all intercourse between persons residing in their territory and persons residing in the territory of the Covenant-breaking State, and the pre-vention of all financial, commercial or personal intercourse between persons residing in the territory of the Covenant-breaking State and persons residing in the territory of any other State, whether a Member of the League or not.

"It is for the Council to give an opinion whether or not a breach of the Covenant has taken place.   In deliberations on this question in the Council, the votes of Members of the League alleged to have

Plan requires that these two Articles (X and
XVI) shall be struck out of the Covenant of the
League; and the eminent jury, in approving of
this proposal, show a very lively sense of the
aversion with which the bulk of the American
people regard any proposal to involve them,
however vaguely and conditionally, in any ob-

---

resorted to war and of Members against whom such action was directed shall not be counted.

"The Council will notify to all Members of the League the date
which it recommends for the application of the economic pressure
under this Article."

It is to be noted that the Council is charged merely with the duty
of *advising*, of giving an *opinion*, of *recommending*, of piously sug-
gesting to the Members of the League that the time for action has
arrived. In its original unamended form Article XVI prescribed:
"It shall be the duty of the Council in such case (breach of covenant)
to *recommend* to the several Governments concerned what effective
military, naval, or air force the Members of the League shall severally
contribute to the armed forces to be used to protect the covenants of
the League." But this right and duty of "recommending" was found
to be too strong meat for the babes of international coöperation and
was therefore amended away.

If we remember that decisions of both the Council and the As-
sembly of the League must be unanimous, and if we duly weigh the
considerations urged by Justice J. H. Clarke (cited in the footnote on
p. 216) is it not obvious that, even if the United States should join
the existing League, the prospect of the League's obtaining the
coöperation of American forces in the prevention of aggression
would be vanishingly small? Is it not probable in the highest
degree that the United States would refuse any such coöperation and
would, at the most, coöperate in the expression of moral censure upon
the threatening or actual aggression? And is there any reasonable
prospect of an effective enforcement of the proposed boycott upon
traders and manufacturers who have learnt that war provides the
greatest opportunity for the rapid acquirement of great wealth?

ligation to take up arms, or to impose the self-denying ordinance of trade-boycott, in defense of any other nation against aggression.

Now Articles X and XVI, though they do little more than involve the Members of the League in a pious avowment of a moral obligation to censure unjustified aggression upon any nation, contain or constitute whatever of effective sanction, whatever "teeth," the existing League can claim. Yet, weak and untrustworthy as are the teeth, it would seem that they must be drawn from the League, before it may reasonably hope for the adhesion of the United States. When the League shall have been emasculated to this degree, its power to protect nations against aggression and to inspire them with the confidence essential to disarmament (which power is, under the existing form of the Covenant, wofully inadequate) will have been reduced to a negligible quantity.

All the more necessary is it, therefore, to adopt the International Air-force plan sketched in the foregoing appendix, in order to give to the World Court the sanction, the power of enforcing its rulings, without which neither the Court nor the League, nor both together, can hope to bring about general disarmament and enduring peace.

The International Air-force plan is, then, in no sense in conflict or rivalry with the Bok Peace Plan. It is rather a much needed, an indispensable, supplement to it. Without the adoption of this supplementary plan, without the effective sanction of the World Court's rulings which this plan would provide, the League and the Court will remain little more than a glorified Red Cross Society and a pious gesture deprecating war and aggression. And, since the adoption of this supplementary plan would avoid involving any nation in the obligation to take up arms or to maintain armed forces of its own, it is difficult to see how the most extreme pacifist or the most convinced opponent of anything that can involve the United States in direct intervention in the affairs of other nations could entertain any serious objection to it.

The only reasonable ground of objection that any sincere and public spirited person could find would be, I think, the extreme Tolstoian doctrine that in no conceivable circumstances is the use or the threat of force morally permissible. Such persons must, if they were consistent, oppose all police action, domestic as well as international;

they must be prepared to look on with what equanimity they can summon, while women and children are brutally assaulted by footpads or murdered wholesale by the hundred thousand in the wars of the future which even now are looming darkly above the international horizon.

I add one word upon the plan actively urged by the *Christian Science Monitor* and now finding widespread support, the plan, namely, of a constitutional amendment which would render obligatory the conscription of all wealth as well as of all persons, in the event of the United States engaging in war. This plan would, if it were adopted, render it more than ever difficult, in fact practically impossible, to secure the coöperation of the United States in any International action for the prevention of unjust aggression. In so far it might prove to be of great injury to the world. But, if it were combined with the adoption of the International Air-force plan, this grave objection to it would be wholly removed, and we might hope to see it adopted with a good conscience by the United States and imitated by other nations.

INDEX

A Selection from the
Catalogue of

G. P. PUTNAM'S SONS

**Complete Catalogues sent
on application**

THE GROUP MIND

A Sketch of the Principles of Collective Psychology with some attempt to apply them to the Interpretation of National Life and Character

BY

WILLIAM McDOUGALL, F.R.S.

Professor of Psychology, Harvard University

Late Fellow of St. John's College, Cambridge, Fellow of Corpus Christi College, and Wilde Reader in Mental Philosophy in the University of Oxford

This volume constitutes the second step in the author's projected *Treatise on Social Psychology*, the first volume of which, *Introduction to Social Psychology*, was published in 1908.

In this new work, the author sketches the principles of the mental life of groups, and applies these principles to the understanding of the life of nations. He hopes that the book may constitute a contribution towards the great experiment in Social Science which the American people is making with so ardent a faith in the power of the Group Mind to attain effective direction of its own development.

G. P. Putnam's Sons

New York   London

The
Problem of Population

By

Harold Cox, M.A.

This book discusses from the economic
and moral points of view the principal aspects of the problem of population, which
affects almost every phase of human life.
Mr. Cox, a world-wide authority on the
subject, shows the demoralising physical
result of over-population, both upon the
individual mother and upon her children.
He then discusses the racial and national
aspects of the problem, and devotes a
final word to the ethics involved in the
conscious limitation of offspring.

G. P. Putnam's Sons

New York   London